CRETE
DEATH FROM THE SKIES

For my father and mother,
uncles and aunts, who
went through the war.

Text © David Filer, 2010
Typographical design © David Bateman Ltd, 2010

Published in 2010 by David Bateman Ltd,
30 Tarndale Grove, Albany, Auckland,
New Zealand

ISBN 978-1-86953-782-1

Editor: Caroline List
Book design: Trevor Newman
Maps: Nick Keenleyside, Outline Draughting &
    Graphics Ltd
Printed in China by Everbest Printing Co. Ltd

CRETE

DEATH FROM THE SKIES

NEW ZEALAND'S ROLE IN THE LOSS OF CRETE

DAVID FILER

David Bateman

Introduction

The battle of Crete, fought in May–June 1941, is unique in military history. It was the first battle to be won by airborne troops alone, who landed on the island by parachute, glider and transport plane. These invaders were Germans (and Austrians), supported at the end by some Italian forces, while the defenders were a mix of New Zealand, Australian, British and Greek troops, backed by the courageous men, women and children of Crete.

Of these peoples, the conflict remains of importance primarily to New Zealanders and Cretans. Kiwi soldiers played a crucial role in the battle and it was their commanders who made the key decisions. New Zealand casualties, with over 3,800 dead, wounded and prisoners of war, were high for such a small country. For their part, the Cretans had to suffer the horrors of a four-year brutal occupation once the battle was over. Although every act of resistance would lead to bloody reprisals, by 1945 the Cretan guerrillas had largely liberated their homeland by themselves.

Many New Zealanders who had refused to surrender when the battle was lost, or who escaped from prison camps, were sheltered by Cretan families. Some spent years on Crete, forming close friendships with their protectors, who risked their lives to hide them. A few would eventually marry Cretan girls and, once the war had ended, would bring them across the seas to live in a more peaceful land.

Understandably then, a strong and special bond was formed between New Zealand and Crete which lasted for many decades after the conflict. Only now, as

Page 2: Kiwi soldiers on Crete. [N.E. Andrews/Filer collection]

Page 4: A soldier fills his water bottle during the retreat. [ATL: DA-08185]

Left: *Today the beaches west of Canea are occupied by tourists and their apartments, not by Allied soldiers.* [David Filer]

Above: Two Cretan shepherds soon after the war's end. [ATL: DA-09985]

the wartime generation dies away, is the relationship fading. Cretans still remember it each year on the 20th of May, when they commemorate the battle on the anniversary of the first day of fighting, but on the other side of the world, the majority of Kiwis now know little about it.

When I first went to Crete as a young student on my 'OE' in 1973, the island was still off the main tourist track and seemed largely unaffected by modern commercial development. I can clearly recall visiting the old defensive walls at Heraklion and the partially rebuilt Minoan palace of Knossos.[1] At that time any Cretan over the age of 40 would have held vivid memories of the 1941 battle and its aftermath.

My wife and I returned 36 years later to see the areas where the New Zealanders had fought and died. As we flew into Canea airport on a lumbering turboprop, I felt our view must be similar to that of the German paratroopers nearly seven decades before. But once on the ground everything seemed changed, as the tourist tsunami that has swamped most of the northern Mediterranean coast had also hit Crete. Canea's ancient harbourside was packed with people from all over the world, particularly northern Europeans who have bought into the holiday apartment boom, and all along the coast where the Kiwi battalions had been based, small villages have been taken over by hotels, condominiums, restaurants and shops.

Only at the war cemeteries did the past come alive. Both the Commonwealth war graves at Suda Bay, where 448 New Zealanders lie[2], and the German cemetery near Maleme are well-maintained oases of quiet reflection in a busy beach and café world. While we were visiting, coaches of Scandinavian tourists arrived at both sites to contemplate the terrible harvest of a war most would not remember. They were not taken to the village of Kondomari, close to Maleme, where a memorial commemorates a monstrous crime, the execution of some 60 Cretan men by the Germans the day after the Allies surrendered.

Cretans have not forgotten and similar memorials can be found in many towns and villages. In Canea there are two museums dedicated to their proud military and naval history along with a small privately run one in Galatas, where the Kiwis fought in hand-to-hand combat with the invaders. While we were in the village square there, yet another tour party arrived.

Back in New Zealand, however, the conflict seems forgotten, except among ageing veterans and the enthusiasts with an interest in our military history. The battle of Crete is not taught in our schools where it seems that the educational establishment thinks that war stories might encourage boys' dreams of glory. And while discussions about Anzac Day are permitted, they are dominated by the Gallipoli campaign of the First World War.

Yet the conflict on Crete is, for New Zealand, the 'Gallipoli' of the Second World War. It is one of the few events in that earth-shattering time when Kiwi troops took centre stage and where, with better leadership, a battle that was lost might have been won. Unlike Gallipoli, however, where British generals made the mistakes that led to defeat, on Crete our own commanders made the crucial blunders. Why they did so is the major theme of this book.

In recent years, works on the Second World War have been increasingly dominated by oral histories of fighting men and civilians recalling some of the most intense moments in their lives. This is part of a worldwide trend to 'people's history', telling the story of great events from the bottom up, an understandable and accessible reaction to too many earlier books focusing on the decisions of politicians, generals and diplomats. Some recent works on the battle of Crete have reflected this approach.[3]

The danger of bottom-up history, however, is that it can ignore the profound impact that the decisions of the powerful have on ordinary people. The choices

Below: The memorial at Kondomari, where German paratroopers executed many villagers in June 1941. [David Filer]

Above: These wounded Kiwis on Crete were photographed using a captured German camera. The man in the middle holds a German pistol. [ATL: PAColl-6677-4]

made by a general will affect the lives or deaths of thousands of common soldiers; the choices of a private will usually affect only his mates. Any substantial analysis of a battle must therefore consider the roles of the commanders (and the politicians behind them), as well as the actions of the fighting men.

I have tried in this book to balance the top-down and bottom-up approaches. The personalities of the various commanders are assessed, as are the reasons for their decisions, while the actions of ordinary soldiers taken in response to those decisions are also described. It is generally agreed that New Zealand soldiers fought well on Crete; the debate is whether their commanders performed as effectively. My argument is that, at critical points, they did not.

It is, of course, much easier to analyse a general's decisions in a chair in front of one's computer than to have to make them in the confusion, stress and danger of a battlefield, and a historian does not carry the responsibility for the lives of thousands of young men. In hindsight too, a writer already knows the enemy's strength, dispositions and plans. As historian and retired Major General Julian Thompson has said: 'It is easy to be wise after the event, pontificating from the calm of a book-lined study. But one has to remember that in war the true state of an opposition's capability is often far from clear.'[4]

Nevertheless, on Crete the commanders knew the German invasion plans in detail before the attack. British Prime Minister Winston Churchill made sure that decoded German signals were communicated to the Allied commander on Crete, the New Zealand general Bernard Freyberg, who then passed the gist on to his subordinates. And yet the battle still was lost, much to Churchill's chagrin. He too, however, played a key role in setting the scene for defeat. Few leaders on either side would come out of this battle with their reputations untarnished.

Since the end of the Second World War a number of books have been produced about the battle of Crete, starting with the magnificent official New Zealand history written by Dan Davin (who served on Crete), which was published in 1953. Other authors have followed, mainly in Britain and New Zealand, with the most prominent and influential being Antony Beevor, whose *Crete: the Battle and the Resistance* was written some 20 years ago. Beevor cemented in the widely held view of British historians that Freyberg was the chief architect of the Allies' defeat, but none of these writers consulted important archives in New Zealand, which suggest other reasons for the debacle. I am very grateful to the small local 'band of brothers' who have gone before me and have unearthed the evidence for alternative positions.

One of the new sources for this book are a number of interviews that I did for the television documentary series *Freyberg V.C.*, which was screened in the mid-1980s. I was lucky enough to speak to many senior officers in New Zealand and overseas who had known Bernard Freyberg, including some who had served on Crete. They all still had strong opinions about the battle. Although the sound tapes of those interviews have been lost, I fortunately kept my copy of the transcripts (and research notes) and have since made sure that further copies have been deposited in the Defence Library in Wellington and the National Army Museum in Waiouru for future use by historians.

This book also presents a pictorial history of the battle. Against regulations, a number of Kiwi soldiers took their own cameras to Greece and Crete and others used cameras appropriated from captured or dead Germans. Many of their photos were later brought together in the War History collection which is now held in the Alexander Turnbull Library (ATL), along with additional German images from Crete. Other pictures are from overseas archives or are ones I have collected myself over the years. Because most of these photos were taken by amateurs, often in the front line, there is a freshness and reality about them that official war photographers struggle to catch.

A new set of images in the book are stills from a colour film shot on Crete by a Kiwi soldier, Major O.G. Wiles.[5] Only a small number of films were made of the battle and these stills are from the only known colour one and, although they are not always in full focus, they offer a unique and significant perspective. I have also included some photos that I took on my tour around the battlefields in 2009, to show how they look today.

Hopefully, this book will lead to New Zealanders thinking afresh about this important event in their history. It might even eventually be taught in school. And some Kiwis may decide to make a pilgrimage to a beautiful island where their forefathers fought and died alongside the brave local people to help defend their independence and their freedoms.

David Filer, 31 March 2010

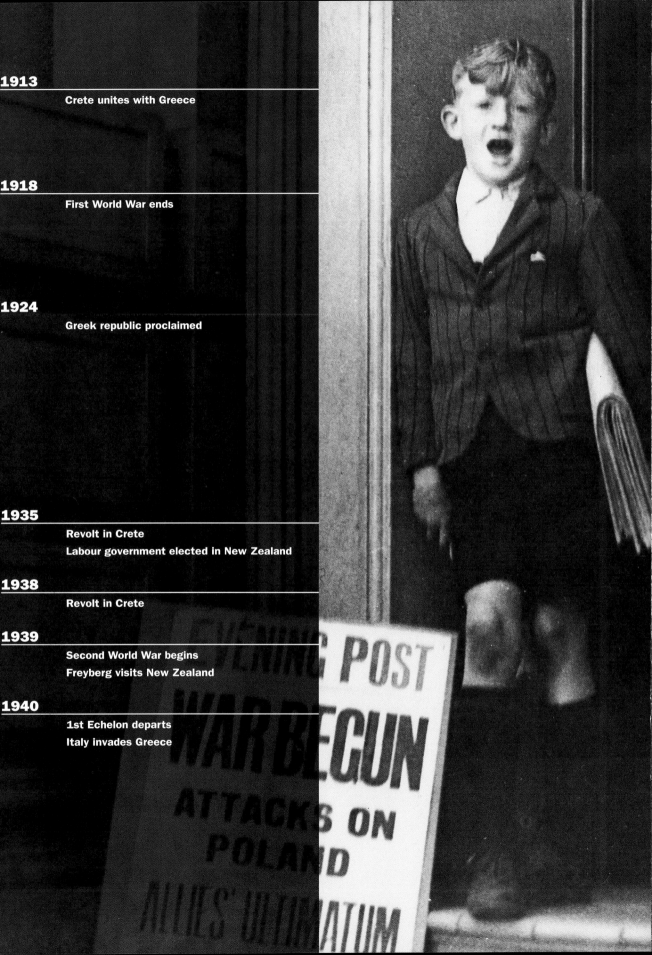

1913

Crete unites with Greece

1918

First World War ends

1924

Greek republic proclaimed

1935

Revolt in Crete
Labour government elected in New Zealand

1938

Revolt in Crete

1939

Second World War begins
Freyberg visits New Zealand

1940

1st Echelon departs
Italy invades Greece

1

PASSAGES TO WAR

Crete is an ancient land, a place of myth and legend, the isle where Zeus was born. There the half-man, half-bull Minotaur stalked his deadly labyrinth, and Icarus took mankind's first flight before soaring too close to the sun. The island was settled at least 9,000 years ago and one of the great early civilisations, the Minoans, flourished there around 2,000 BC.

Previous page: A newspaper boy in Wellington in September 1939.
[ATL: Detail of 1/2-66962-F]

Below left: The harbour at Canea, showing the Venetian walls and lighthouse. [David Filer]

Below right: A bas-relief portraying Cretan fighters. [Hotel Doma, Canea]

Crete's strategic location in the eastern Mediterranean also made it the focus of other people's ambitions. The German invasion in May 1941 was just the last in a long line of similar tragedies. After the Minoan civilisation declined, Dorians from mainland Greece occupied the island, to be followed by Romans, the Bystantine Empire, Arabs, Venetians and Turks. Each left their imprint, as well as creating a long tradition of resistance by Cretans to foreign domination.

While most of Greece was part of the empire of the Ottoman Turks from the middle of the fifteenth century, Crete was not conquered until 1669. There were regular rebellions against Turkish rule, both on the mainland and the islands. One of the most significant occurred in Crete in 1770 when Ioannis Vlachos, a merchant better known as Daskalogiannis, led an uprising based in the port of Sfakia. New Zealand soldiers would come to know this town and its beaches and hinterland well over a few stressful days in mid-1941.

The Sfakia revolt was suppressed and Daskalogiannis was cruelly executed, although his memory lives on, with the modern international airport at Canea named after him.

Fifty years after his death the Greek War of Independence began with a widespread, popular revolt against the oppressive overlords. After Britain, France and Russia intervened, the Turks were driven out of much of the mainland and in 1832 a new Greek state was founded. But Crete was not included and largely remained under Turkish control, despite ongoing uprisings and bloody reprisals. Eventually the Great Powers again intervened and, after a few years of semi-independence, Crete was united with Greece in 1913.

This long history of struggle and separation explains why proud independence is a defining feature of the Cretan character; Cretans see themselves as different, as more resilient and resourceful than other Greeks. Zorba, the central character in the famous film (based on the equally well-known novel by Cretan writer Nikos Kazantzakis), is called 'the Greek' because, as a mainlander on Crete, he is an outsider.

Cretans also have a strong history of republican sentiment. They despised the Greek king, George II (a first cousin of Prince Philip, Duke of Edinburgh) who, after a brief reign, had been deposed in the 1920s. So when a military dictator in Athens restored the monarchy in 1935, the Cretans rose in an unsuccessful revolt. Three years later another rebellion followed, this time against a new dictator, the Greek fascist Ioannis Metaxas. This uprising was also suppressed and many of the rifles and pistols commonly owned by Cretans at that time were confiscated by government forces. One unforeseen outcome was that the local people would lack modern weapons and the jails would still be crowded with patriots when the German invasion occurred.

Before this battle opened, however, there would be two earlier invasions of mainland Greece, instigated by the arrogant Italian dictator, Benito Mussolini. This vain, bombastic man was desperate to create a new Roman empire. He had begun his campaign by invading Abyssinia (present-day Ethiopia) in 1935, and four years later turned his gaze closer to home, towards Albania. Italy already had considerable influence over Albania's economy and government, despite the resistance of its uniquely named king, Zog I. Control over Albania would allow the Italians to dominate the Adriatic Sea and thus put pressure on Greece.

After an ultimatum was rejected, Mussolini sent his troops into Albania on 7 April 1939 and despite some resistance, the small, backward country was conquered in less than a week. Zog and his family fled and Italian soldiers now stood on the border of northern Greece.

Halfway round the globe most New Zealanders knew nothing of the Cretan resistance to dictatorship or of Mussolini's invasion of Albania. Their immediate concerns were domestic, as New Zealand continued its slow climb out of the mire of the Great Depression, and the first Labour government introduced the brave new world of social security. If Kiwis were worried about the rise of fascism in Europe, it was more about Nazi Germany and the threat that Adolf Hitler's dreams and ambitions might lead to another world war.

As in most democracies, the New Zealand government was focused on economic and social development, not on military affairs and rearmament. Spending on the armed forces had declined after 1930 and soon the army was on a slippery slope to ruin. It was made up of a small Regular force, the professional soldiers, and a much larger group of part-timers, the Territorials. When compulsory military training was suspended in 1930 the numbers in the Territorial force collapsed. Howard Kippenberger (who would play a pivotal role during the battle of Crete) later recalled this unhappy period:

The period 1930–38 was probably the most discouraging the New Zealand Army has survived. Those who soldiered on, Regular or Territorial, knew they had no support or sympathy from Government or the great majority of the public. . . . Few firms found it possible to spare the services of even the most junior office boy to do any training, unless of course he would forgo his pay. Most officers used their annual leave in attending camps or courses. Equipment was never replaced, however worn or useless.[1]

By the mid-1930s the country which had sent 99,000 men to the First World War would have been hard pressed to raise a force of 3,000. As late as April 1939, the New Zealand army was so under strength that 'there was doubt whether it could have provided without notice a unit of 500 well-equipped men for Singapore'.[2]

Yet the dogs of war were awake and barking. New Zealanders may have failed to notice the Italian occupation of Albania, but they were aware of Nazi aggression in central Europe. In October 1938, after the British and French governments had given in to Hitler, German forces occupied the Sudetenland region of Czechoslovakia (the western borderlands where some ethnic Germans lived). In one of the most famous foolish statements in history, British Prime Minister Neville Chamberlain proclaimed 'peace in our time'. But only six months later German troops were marching into Bohemia and Moravia, thus completing the dismemberment of Czechoslovakia.

Britain now began to prepare for what seemed an inevitable war with Germany, and most of the Dominions (the self-governing countries in the British Commonwealth) reluctantly followed suit. In New Zealand the Labour Government agreed to increase the numbers in the Territorials, although it would not commit to sending an expeditionary force overseas if war was declared. Labour may have hated the rise of fascism in Europe, but it had been opposed to conscription and militarism for decades and could not easily reverse its views.

Right: Recruiting for the 1st Echelon of 2NZEF outside the Central Post Office in Auckland. [ATL: DA-07094]

Far right: Bernard Freyberg and Peter Fraser (Italy, 1944). [ATL: DA-03251]

Map: Eastern Mediterranean.

Suddenly, everything changed. Two days after the German invasion of Poland on 1 September 1939, Britain declared war on Germany (as did New Zealand) and the Second World War began. Prime Minister Michael Joseph Savage spoke for most New Zealanders when he said 'where Britain goes, we go', and within a few days the government had agreed to despatch a 'Special Force' to assist the war effort in Europe.

This force would be called the 2nd New Zealand Expeditionary Force (2NZEF) and its main fighting unit would be the 2nd New Zealand Division. But first it had to be recruited, equipped and trained and, with a weakened foundation to build on, this would take time.

A big question was, who would command 2NZEF and the division. Most of the senior officers in New Zealand had last fought in the First World War and since then had seen little of modern strategy and tactics. Their units had continued to rely on horses, not tanks and vehicles, and lacked up-to-date artillery and anti-aircraft guns. It seemed sensible to look for someone overseas, in particular, a senior commander in the British army.

By late 1939 Savage was very ill (he was dying of cancer) and his tough, clever deputy, Peter Fraser, was making the key decisions about the war effort. When he was in London in November 1939 he arranged to meet a famous Kiwi expatriate and soldier, Bernard Freyberg, who had served in the British forces from 1914 and had risen to the rank of major general.

Freyberg had offered his services to the New Zealand government in the first

GENERAL FREYBERG

Bernard Freyberg's story is very much a Kiwi one, the self-made man rising from obscurity to prominence on the international stage. He was born in Britain in 1889, but arrived in Wellington with his parents and brothers two years later. Although much of his life would be spent on the other side of the world, his formative years — from the age of two to twenty-five — took place in New Zealand.

Freyberg was a champion swimmer in his youth and, at 1.8 metres tall and with a broad chest, was inevitably nicknamed 'Tiny'. His initial career was as a dentist, but he was also an enthusiastic officer in the Territorial force. In March 1914 he left New Zealand, purportedly to further his dental education but really in search of adventure and, when the First World War began, he dashed to England to join up.

In London he enlisted in the newly formed Royal Naval Division, a step which would transform his life. As a lieutenant in the Hood battalion, he joined the social, intellectual and political elite of England, for its officers were the cream of 'Oxbridge'. Among them were Rupert Brooke, the most famous poet of the time, and Arthur Asquith, a son of the prime minister.

The First World War made Freyberg a household name. He proved himself a courageous, resourceful and resilient leader and at the age of 28 he reportedly was the youngest general in the British army. He served in the Antwerp expedition in 1914, at Gallipoli the following year, and through some of the worst battles on the Western Front. For conspicuous bravery during the battle of the Ancre in 1916, he was awarded the Victoria Cross.

Freyberg was also extremely lucky. By the of the Armistice he had been wounded nine times and many of his friends and relatives had been killed. He wrote at the time:

Right: Freyberg in the 1920s. [ATL: 1/1-015216-G]

Far right: The dining room of the New Zealand Forces Club in the palatial Hotel Baglioni in Florence. [ATL: DA-07665]

'I only know it wasn't my fault I am alive.'[3] After the war he joined the British regular army as a captain in the Grenadier Guards, and in 1922 became part of a notable English family when he married Barbara McLaren, niece of the famous gardener, Gertrude Jekyll.

He rose rapidly up the army list in the interwar years and by 1934 was a major general, but the following year he was diagnosed with a heart murmur and had to reluctantly retire. He was recalled to the colours in September 1939, proved himself fit for active service, and became the commander of 2NZEF.

From April 1941 to May 1945 Freyberg led the New Zealanders through campaigns in Greece, Crete, North Africa and Italy. While the division was forged into a highly effective fighting force, he was acutely conscious that he was in command of much of the youth of a small country and that they should not be sacrificed in a single action. This may have made him more cautious than other more bloody-minded generals.

Freyberg's concern for the welfare of his men was reflected in the establishment of soldiers' clubs in Egypt and Italy, staffed by Kiwi women working under the kindly supervision of his wife. As he grew to know his men, his appreciation of them and affection for them increased, which they often reciprocated.

After the war Freyberg became a popular governor-general of New Zealand and in 1951 was raised to the peerage. On returning to England he was appointed Deputy Constable and Lieutenant-Governor of Windsor Castle. It was fitting that he eventually died of a war wound, when an aorta damaged on Gallipoli in 1915 ruptured at Windsor nearly five decades later.

GENERAL FREYBERG

days of the war and when Fraser met him at the Savoy Hotel, he quickly took to this big man with his commanding presence and wide military knowledge. Fraser was struck 'not only by his personality and by his obvious experience and confidence, but particularly by the supreme importance which he clearly attached to the proper treatment of the troops'.[4] He discussed appointing Freyberg to lead 2NZEF with General Ironside, the Chief of the Imperial General Staff, and recorded the positive response:

> He at once made it plain that in his opinion we could not make a better choice. He also spoke in the highest terms of Freyberg, whom he had known for a very lengthy period, and he expressed the opinion that Freyberg invariably took care of his men even at the risk of his own safety.[5]

Winston Churchill, then First Lord of the Admiralty, who had been friends with Freyberg for many years, also supported his candidacy. Fraser telegraphed his own recommendation to Wellington and the government duly offered the command of 2NZEF to Freyberg, which he immediately accepted. So the die was cast, and Kiwi soldiers would later be grateful to find that Ironside's opinions were largely accurate.

Freyberg now had to take part in all the major decisions about the structure, deployment and training of the expeditionary force and the division, which he also commanded. Two weeks later he set off for New Zealand, flying via Egypt, where the Kiwis were to equip and train for a modern war. During a brief stop he chose Maadi, a pleasant town outside Cairo, as the main base for 2NZEF, and by the end of the war 76,000 Kiwis would pass through it.

The new commander arrived in New Zealand on Christmas Day 1939, not to a holiday but to a hectic round of meetings, inspections and civic receptions. Volunteers had been pouring into the expeditionary force offices and the troopships carrying the first contingent (the '1st Echelon') were to leave in just twelve days, with their general on board. While Freyberg was concerned about the soldiers' level of training, he had deeper reservations about some of the senior officers who had been provisionally appointed to lead the division. They were all decorated First World War veterans, but some already seemed too old and most were part-timers short on command experience. The key positions were the brigadiers, especially the heads of the three infantry brigades.

Edward Puttick, a Regular soldier, had been appointed commander of the 4th Infantry Brigade. A well-known journalist who met Puttick just before the fighting on Crete described him as 'a talkative man apt to fuss over trifles', but added 'he had plenty of courage and knew his trade'.[6] Harold Barrowclough, a prominent lawyer, would later take charge of the 6th Brigade. He would perform well during the actions on Greece, but his troops would miss the battle of Crete.

Freyberg's main concern was over who would command the other infantry brigade, a position sought by Southland farmer and member of parliament (MP), James Hargest. It appeared, however, that this nuggety little man was still suffering from the effects of his service in the First World War 20 years before. During that terrible conflict, doctors had worked out that soldiers could experience severe physical and psychological trauma from being under intense shellfire, even if they were not actually wounded. They called it 'shell shock' and noted that among its long-term effects were mood swings, confusion, inertia and depression.

Since the war Hargest had appeared to occasionally succumb to shell shock and in 1939 a medical board concluded that he was unfit for overseas service. But as a senior Territorial officer, he desperately wanted to go and, although he was an

Below left: Freyberg and his brigadiers in Egypt. Left to right: Puttick, Freyberg, British general Sir John Dill, Hargest and Barrowclough. [ATL: DA-01141]

Below right: Members of the 1st Echelon wave farewell. [ATL: DA-07124]

Opposition MP, he appealed directly to Peter Fraser. The result was that despite Freyberg's reluctance, Hargest was eventually confirmed in the job. His wife wrote to Fraser, 'I know that your intervention and firm stand on his behalf saved him from becoming a broken man . . . I am glad that he is to go. Even a broken body is better than a broken heart.'[7] The New Zealand Chief of Staff told Freyberg: 'This was a Government decision, and they took all responsibility from myself and the D.M.S. [Director of Medical Services].'[8]

It remains unclear why Fraser backed Hargest. The acting prime minister had only limited experience of military matters and no doubt Hargest (who had offered to assist the government soon after the declaration of war) was persuasive. Perhaps Fraser wanted a political informant, someone who was beholden to him, at the highest levels of 2NZEF; on the other hand he may simply have felt sorry for his parliamentary colleague. In relation to the battle of Crete, however, this would prove a fateful decision.

As the new commander of a national force, Freyberg also had to sort out his formal relationship with the government. This was embodied in a charter which gave him the right to discuss with the government any matters concerning the employment of the expeditionary force. This meant he would be able to refer disagreements with senior British commanders to New Zealand for Ministers to resolve, if necessary at the highest political level. His newly appointed personal assistant, John White, noted this significant power:

> I remember at that time thinking, well here was a man who was taking the expeditionary force away under his command and very much as a Roman consul might well have taken the legions of Rome. The powers were set out in detail but there was a special power . . . that in the event of there being an emergency or special circumstances of which he was to be the judge, he had the right to refer the matter to the New Zealand government direct.'[9]

Right: A troopship departs Lyttelton for the Middle East.

[ATL: DA-07119]

Left: Winston Churchill takes the salute from D Company of the Maori Battalion in England in 1940. [ATL: DA-07430]

Freyberg was willing to use this power, but initially he did not understand also how fully informed the government wanted to be. This would cause grave misunderstandings and threaten his position after the fall of Greece and Crete.

But these problems were in the future and on 6 January an exhausted general sailed from New Zealand in the convoy carrying the 6,500 men of the 1st Echelon to Egypt. Immediately after arrival he faced another busy round of settling in his troops, establishing headquarters and beginning a rigorous training regime.

The next echelon, including Hargest and the 5th Brigade, was due to arrive in Egypt in May, but concerns about a potential threat from the Italian air force in Abyssinia led to the convoy being diverted, first to Cape Town, and then on to Scotland. The threat was real as Mussolini, having seen the recent success of Hitler's blitzkrieg in Europe, declared war on Britain and France in early June. Freyberg decided to join the Kiwis in Britain, explaining to the New Zealand government that 'none of my senior officers with the second echelon bound for England is fit to start training without being trained himself'.[10] Soon he was preparing the Kiwis to face a possible German invasion, while along the way ensuring that Winston Churchill, now the prime minister and voice of the nation, inspected his men.

Below: Kiwi soldiers take a break while training in Egypt.
[ATL: Detail of DA-00551]

Meanwhile, a heavily escorted 3rd Echelon reached the Suez Canal and the men were swiftly absorbed into the partially formed division. With the invasion threat declining in Britain, and Italian forces advancing into Egypt, Freyberg took the long flight back to Cairo (including surviving a crash landing in Malta). He resisted his division being used piecemeal against the Italians and so the Kiwis, unlike the Aussies, missed out on the rout of Mussolini's troops.

Freyberg had now addressed most of the officers in 2NZEF, both in Britain and Egypt. To many, he seemed and sounded like a proper 'pom', as the first impressions of Charles Bennett, an officer in the Maori Battalion, indicate:

I expected to see a chap who had some kind of New Zealand characteristic, either by looks or by way of speech or something like that, but there was no sign of a New Zealander in the first Freyberg that I knew. He was a real pukka officer straight from the British army in India . . . that type of bloke, moustache and all, too. So that one's first reaction was, by jove, this chap doesn't seem to be a New Zealander, I hope he'll do alright with the New Zealanders.[11]

Eventually Freyberg would become a 'born again' Kiwi, but these were early days. Other officers were worried by his meddling manner. Freyberg rightly regarded himself as an expert on unit administration, having written a well-received manual on the subject while in the British army. A number of New Zealand subordinates, however, including Hargest, felt he interfered too much in the little matters and excluded them from the bigger picture. His chief administrative officer later wrote:

Altogether it was an uneasy settling-down period, and no one was very happy. We could not fathom the General's mind; and I am sure that to some degree he had lost confidence in himself, and was groping for the best way to handle this new body of men with, at least in part, a different set of values from the men of the mother country.[12]

Below left: Greek soldiers in action on the Albanian front. [War Museum, Canea]

Below right: Bringing up supplies for the Greek forces. [War Museum, Canea]

Freyberg did not help these perceptions with his unusual way of running the conferences he held with commanders and staff. He would often start by throwing around some broad, contradictory, even outlandish ideas and, pushing for reactions, would create doubt and confusion. Later it would be clear that he was using his officers as a sounding board to test all possibilities and was trying to make them think outside the box.

But initially it seemed odd, and behaviour like this may explain why some senior British officers regarded him as a 'bear of little brain'. Historian Antony Beevor states that Freyberg's 'obstinacy and lack of comprehension were something of a

joke amongst his fellow generals', and suggests these were one explanation for the decisions he would take on Crete.[13]

In fact, Freyberg was an intelligent man but poorly educated in comparison to many of his British counterparts who had gone to military college or to university. He was aware of this and had toyed with enrolling at Oxford's Balliol College just after the end of the First World War, but instead chose to stay in the army. The Rhodes scholars and other bright graduates, however, who served on his staff in the next war had no doubts as to his intellect or curiosity. One of them, Geoffrey Cox, later described meeting him:

> His powerful frame seemed to fill the tent, but his face, with wide-set eyes which studied me sharply, had something boyish about it, alert as well as strong with a hint of humour, even of mischievousness in its lines. It was also the face of a man of keen intelligence.[14]

In any event, the officers and men of the New Zealand Division were about to move from theoretical discussions, petty gripes and never-ending training to active service. By early 1941 the 2nd Echelon was finally sailing from Britain to join its brothers-in-arms, and a bitter battle had begun in the freezing mountains of northern Greece.

Once Albania was conquered, Mussolini had set his sights on adding Greece to his new Roman empire, despite an ambivalent attitude by his ally, Adolf Hitler. From mid-1940 Italian propaganda and acts of provocation against the Greeks had increased and when the Germans occupied Romania's oilfields in October, Mussolini decided to attack south without consulting the Führer. So began a war within the wider world war, initially involving only Italy and Greece but not the German or British armies.

On 28 October 1940 the Italian forces crossed the Albanian border and advanced into northern Greece. Opposition to the Metaxas dictatorship was forgotten as the Greek people united to defend their country. Men flocked to the recruiting offices and the army divisions moved up to the front, among them the Cretan 5th Division which landed at Salonika in November and then marched west to the mountainous region where the war was being fought.

The Italians' initial progress soon came to a halt as the weather closed in, the few tracks turned into quagmires and the air force was grounded. The Greek army then launched a series of counter-attacks which drove their enemies back across the border, and by Christmas most of southern Albania was in Greek hands. Conditions for the soldiers on both sides were terrible, as equipment and clothing fell apart in one of the worst winters on record. The troops suffered from cold, hunger and frostbite, but Greek morale was much higher than that of the invaders and their generals were better prepared.

The Cretan division played its part, smashing an Italian force before exhaustion and stalemate set in during February 1941. By this point, however, greater powers were becoming involved, with both Hitler and Churchill considering sending their armies to join the conflict. In Britain's case this meant finding available units amongst its widely stretched forces, with one of the obvious ones being the 2nd New Zealand Division.

1940
OCTOBER

Italy invades Greece

NOVEMBER

RAF squadron sent to Greece

Greek forces enter Albania

DECEMBER

1941
JANUARY

Metaxas dies

FEBRUARY

MARCH

New Zealand troops arrive in Greece

New Zealand Division in northern Greece

APRIL

German invasion of Yugoslavia and Greece

Battle in the Pinios Gorge
Evacuation of Allies from Greece

MAY

2

A GREEK
TRAGEDY

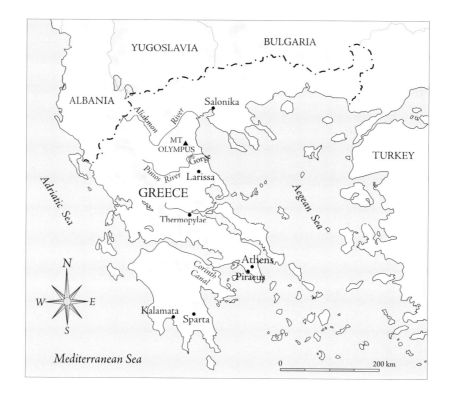

Previous page: *Kiwi
soldiers during the
retreat in Greece.*
[ATL: DA-03564]

*Map: Key locations in
the Greek campaign,
1941.*

**As early as April 1939, when Mussolini's army invaded Albania, the British
government had offered to guarantee Greek independence. London was worried
about German and Italian ambitions in southern Europe and the threat they
could pose to British interests in the Mediterranean, especially the sea routes
through the Suez Canal.**

*Below: Churchill and
Roosevelt (Washington
DC, 1942).* [ATL: Detail of
1/2-036990-F]

When the Italians advanced into Greece eighteen months later, the Greek
government invoked the guarantee, initially seeking support from only
the Royal Air Force (RAF) and the Royal Navy. The British air commander in
the Middle East immediately sent a bomber
squadron, stating that 'it seems that it has
become politically absolutely necessary to send a
token force to Greece even at the expense of my
forces here'.[1]

This was the nub of the problem which would
eventually lead to disaster for the Allied forces
sent to Greece, including the 2nd New Zealand
Division. There were strong political reasons
to support the Greeks, but Britain did not have
the resources to do so effectively. However,
Churchill's government agreed to despatch a
further four RAF squadrons once airfields were

Left: Freyberg addressing New Zealand troops after their arrival in Egypt. Behind him is Anthony Eden, Britain's foreign secretary from late-1940 to 1945. [ATL: DA-00506]

prepared in the south of the country. This first foray into Greece, oddly named 'Barbarity Force', included some men from a New Zealand railway survey company who had been working in Palestine. The New Zealand government was not amused that 2NZEF headquarters had not been informed about this move, and insisted on proper consultation in future.

But Churchill was looking at the bigger picture. He was hoping to form a Balkan front against the Axis powers — Italy, Germany and their smaller allies in central Europe. In 1915, as First Lord of the Admiralty, he had conceived the daring but ill-fated attempt by the Royal Navy to storm the Dardanelles, seize Constantinople (present-day Istanbul) and knock Turkey out of the war (a brainwave which in turn led to the equally disastrous land campaign on the Gallipoli peninsula, where the Anzac legend was born). Despite that failure, Churchill carried into the next world war the belief that the lands along the Mediterranean formed a 'soft underbelly' through which Britain's enemies in central Europe could be attacked.

In 1940, however, Turkey and Yugoslavia were neutral and, despite a flurry of diplomatic activity, showed little enthusiasm for joining the Allies against the Axis. Even the Greek government was worried that the British presence might provoke Hitler into attacking its country. The Führer, having conquered most of Western Europe, was now turning his thoughts eastwards, towards his ideological enemy, the Soviet Union, and a massive assault to destroy it. He could not afford an unresolved conflict on his southern flank, particularly as the Romanian oilfields, essential to his war effort, would be within the range of British bombers in Greece.

Below: Fraser and Wavell (Egypt, 1941). [ATL: Detail of DA-01094B]

Churchill was aware that the Germans were planning an attack on Greece and was considering how to counter it. On his mind, too, was another seemingly distant but related issue, the views of the people and politicians of the United States of America. A beleaguered Britain desperately needed more economic and military aid from the USA and, although President Roosevelt was sympathetic, many Americans wanted to keep out of European affairs. Churchill knew that if Britain were to appear defeatist or unwilling to help threatened nations like Greece, then American opinion could turn increasingly negative. So, in a radio broadcast in early 1941, partly aimed at an American audience, he declared:

> We shall not fail or falter; we shall not weaken or tire. Neither the sudden shock of battle, nor the longdrawn trials of vigilance or exertion will wear us down. Give us the tools and we will finish the job.[2]

Unfortunately, in the Middle East, his forces were short of both tools and men, and the army commander, General Archibald Wavell, was being pulled in all directions. Although the Italians had been hammered in Libya, the British advance had stopped short of the port of Tripoli, through which German reinforcements were soon arriving (along with their commander, the brilliant Erwin Rommel). British soldiers were also fighting the Italians in the east African colonies, and there were threats from Arab nationalists in Iraq and from the Vichy French regime in Syria. It seemed there was little left to aid the Greeks.

This had mattered less while Metaxas remained in charge in Greece, as he was unwilling to accept a token force, but at the end of January 1941 he died of throat cancer and the new prime minister, Alexandros Koryzis, was more receptive to British assistance. So Churchill decided to send his Foreign Secretary, Anthony Eden, along with senior military and diplomatic advisors to Athens for detailed discussions. When the Greeks promised to strongly resist if the Germans invaded, an enthusiastic Eden responded by offering greater support than was actually available. He then hurried off to Ankara to try, unsuccessfully, to bring the Turks into the anti-Axis alliance.

Wavell, meantime, had to find some soldiers to send to Greece. The only units available were two Australian divisions, a Polish brigade, a British armoured brigade and the 2nd New Zealand Division. Britain then decided to consult the Australian and New Zealand governments about using their forces in this uncertain venture.

Unfortunately, Freyberg had recently sent a signal to Wellington stating that the division was about to come together and that 'should the British Government request the release of the New Zealand Expeditionary Force for a full operational role the New Zealand Government can now do so with confidence'.[3] The War Cabinet took this as an endorsement of the Greek proposal and agreed to the despatch of the Kiwis. In fact, Freyberg had serious misgivings about the whole operation, but failed to communicate these views to Fraser who, with Savage's death, was now prime minister.

In any event, the New Zealand government soon had doubts about the size of the Allied force being sent to Greece and the support it would receive. On 26 February Fraser informed London that the government felt 'that the task confronting an

expedition of the size proposed is a most formidable and hazardous one'.[4] A few days later, when they heard that the plan to counter a German invasion had been changed (because of disagreements about the placement of the British and Greek divisions), their response was that an already 'highly dangerous and speculative' plan had been replaced by one 'obviously much more hazardous'.[5] Yet Cabinet still agreed to the New Zealanders going to Greece, while urging that evacuation plans be prepared in case it all went wrong. Their concerns would soon be justified.

On 6 March 1941, only three days after the 5th Brigade had finally reached Egypt, Freyberg and the advance elements of the New Zealand Division set sail from Alexandria, arriving at the port of Piraeus the following day. The units assembled outside Athens and some soldiers were allowed into the city, including a then unknown junior officer, Charles Upham. He later described how the Kiwis came close to causing a diplomatic incident:

> There was a German embassy in Athens with swastikas hanging out the front when we were there. They were looking out the windows and our fellows were getting drunk and climbing up and pulling down their flag . . . I remember one fellow that stole some pyjamas out of the embassy . . . when our fellows sort of raided it.[6]

Above: New Zealand soldiers arrive at Piraeus harbour in Greece. [ATL: DA-10647]

THE 2ND NEW ZEALAND DIVISION

The main fighting formation of 2NZEF was the 2nd New Zealand Division. It was based on the standard British infantry division but, as a national force, it had additional supporting units. In the field it could range in size from 15,000 to 20,000 men.

The division was divided into three infantry *brigades* (each numbering some 3,000 men), with three *battalions* in each brigade (and up to 800 men in each battalion). The battalions were broken down into five *companies* ('A', 'B', 'C', 'D' and Headquarters) — each respectively made up of three 30-man *platoons*. The smallest unit was the *section*, with three of them to a platoon.

In addition to the nine infantry battalions in the division, there was a medium machine-gun battalion and a further infantry battalion for the Maori volunteers, which was attached to various brigades as required.

The normal infantry weapons were the Lee-Enfield bolt-action rifle, the Bren light machine gun, the grenade and the bayonet.

The main arm supporting the infantry was the artillery with three field regiments firing the 25-pounder gun, plus anti-tank and anti-aircraft units. There was also a regiment of Divisional Cavalry, who had given up their horses for Bren-gun carriers and armoured cars. Later in the war, the division would add light and medium tanks.

Beside the fighting units stood engineering, transport, signals and ammunition companies, along with ordnance workshops, field ambulances and medical services. Each unit had its own headquarters and administrative staff and above them all was the divisional headquarters.

While 2NZEF was the successor to 1ZNEF which had gone overseas in the First World War, the nomenclature of the other units was not connected to that war. The 2nd Division followed on from the New Zealand-based 1st Division which, with its three infantry brigades, was for home defence. This meant that the brigades of the 2nd Division would be called the 4th, 5th and 6th. Similarly, with seventeen Territorial infantry regiments already on the books, the nine new battalions were numbered from '18' to '26', with the machine-gun battalion being the 27th and the Maori battalion the 28th.

Making all the units work together was an immense task for Freyberg and his staff and commanders, and required detailed planning and intensive training. In battle the 2nd New Zealand Division formed a huge, powerful force, often much larger than the divisions of other allied nations or their German and Italian opponents.

Below: Soldiers of the New Zealand Division on parade at Maadi camp, Egypt.

[ATL: DA-00657]

Left: A train takes New Zealand soldiers up to the Aliakmon line in Greece. [ATL: DA-08170]

Before any more trouble could result, the division was heading north by road and rail to take up positions near the Aliakmon River. The men dug in, unsure when the attack might come, and even as they prepared their defences, Freyberg was firming up possible lines of retreat behind them.

Matters were suddenly brought to a head in Yugoslavia, a country deeply divided between its various nationalities and pro-German and British factions. On 27 March, two days after the Yugoslav prime minister and regent had signed a pact with Hitler, they were overthrown by a coup d'etat in Belgrade. For a brief period Churchill and Eden could dream that their southern alliance was coming to fruition. But the coup had infuriated Hitler and he ordered the immediate destruction of Yugoslavia, along with the invasion of Greece.

The Germans quickly assembled a huge force for the assault, with 28 army divisions available and their air force (the Luftwaffe) providing some 800 aircraft. The Greeks faced the attack with their battle-hardened but poorly equipped army, mainly opposing the Italians in Albania or scattered along the eastern frontier, along with one Australian and one New Zealand division and a British armoured brigade. There were only 80 serviceable Allied aircraft, and the other Australian division and the Polish brigade had not been sent because Rommel was now advancing in Libya.

On 6 April German soldiers crossed into Yugoslavia and moved through Bulgaria into Greece. The million-strong Yugoslav army, armed with antiquated weapons and rent with disagreements, soon collapsed and the German forces, which

Right: Soldiers from the 21st Battalion in northern Greece.
[ATL: DA-11862]

had suffered fewer than 600 casualties, now struck into central Greece. On the morning of 10 April an advancing column was fired on by New Zealand armoured cars, as the division finally went into action more than nineteen months after the declaration of war. But with the Germans threatening their flanks, other Kiwi units were already pulling back.

The 4th and 5th brigades took up defensive positions in the passes around Mount Olympus, with the 21st Battalion, commanded by Auckland lawyer Lieutenant Colonel 'Polly' Macky, dug in along the coast. His men felt the common anxiety of all the New Zealand soldiers awaiting their first combat with:

> . . . sweat on the palms of their hands and, while every man wondered how he would show up in his first action, many a man was probably thinking, 'I mustn't let my cobbers down, I mustn't let my cobbers down.'[7]

The battalion faced a massive German attack but, supported by Kiwi gunners, they delayed the advance and then withdrew south to the Pinios Gorge. Here their defences were poorly sited and a road demolition left unprotected, allowing the Germans to repair it. As the tanks rolled towards them, some New Zealand and Australian infantrymen broke and began to retreat. The battalion then fell back in confusion and, following Macky's pre-battle advice, dispersed into smaller groups and retreated through the hills.

Other New Zealand units moved back in better order, but the Germans continued to press hard, constantly threatening to cut off the retreating men. Howard Kippenberger, the pre-war small-town lawyer who was now a rising star in the division, was bringing back a demolition party when enemy vehicles blocked its route. He had to lead his men over open country, with the Germans close by, before he reached the relative safety of the New Zealand lines. Meanwhile Bernard Freyberg was in his element, visiting commanders, rapidly revising plans, encouraging his exhausted men and, at one point, even directing traffic through the crossroads at Larissa.

Air attacks were increasing, as the Luftwaffe, now operating from airfields in northern Greece, took command of the skies. Freyberg had a number of cars shot up by low-flying German fighters while he toured around the troops. His driver Laurie Cropp recalled one such attack:

> We were strafed by a team of Messerschmitts that used to do the roads up every evening. The first burst seemed to hit the car and the windscreen creamed. I pulled up and everybody in the car lay down where possible, and it seemed that the car was being torn to bits but this was only the gravel off the road. The first one to move was the General who opened the back door and got into a ditch by the side of the road and we all followed.[8]

The Kiwis soon withdrew to strong positions in the Thermopylae area, where Leonidas and the 300 Spartans had made their immortal stand against the Persians some two and a half millennia earlier. But the Greek military and government were now in chaos, with the Germans having smashed through their defence lines and trapped the army (including the Cretan division) on the Albanian front. On 18 April, as the king and cabinet considered abandoning Athens, a distraught prime minister left the room, took out a revolver and shot himself.

Three days later Wavell ordered the evacuation of the British and Commonwealth troops. Unfortunately, the final withdrawal had not been properly prepared and

Below left: An injured German soldier lies beside his tank after it struck a mine in the Mount Olympus area. [ATL: DA-11612]

Below right: One of Freyberg's cars after an attack by a German aircraft. [Sir John White]

Freyberg later complained that 'no evacuation plan had been made, or apparently even considered, until we were almost back on the beaches'.[9]

On Anzac Day the Royal Navy picked up the 5th Brigade from beaches east of Athens and carried it to Crete, while the 6th and 4th brigades headed for ports in the Peloponnese region. The former group got across the bridge over the Corinth Canal (which the Allies were preparing to blow up), but before the other brigade arrived, German aircraft massed over the waterway. New Zealand infantry and engineers near by saw for the first time the airborne forces they would soon face on Crete, with the Luftwaffe transport planes:

> . . . flying low in groups of three to drop the many-coloured parachutes supporting the troopers and their supplies. At the same time gliders crash-landed near the bridge, the men from its south end rushing on to clear the demolitions.[10]

But as the Germans were removing the charges the whole bridge blew up, for reasons which are still unclear,[11] and the wreckage dropped into the canal. The 4th Brigade now had to turn south and were fortunate to later be uplifted from the coast near Athens and taken to Crete. Meanwhile the 6th Brigade withdrew to beaches below Sparta where, after a day of great anxiety, they were eventually collected by the Royal Navy to sail first for Crete and then on to Egypt.

Not all the New Zealanders got away. The troops who had been sent to 'Calamity

Bay' — Kalamata — in the southern Peloponnese could not be evacuated and, despite a brief battle in which Jack Hinton showed the courage which won him the Victoria Cross, most were captured. Of the 16,700 Kiwis who went to Greece, 1,826 were taken prisoner, while 291 were killed and 387 wounded. The British, Australian and Greek forces also suffered significant casualties.

Furthermore, a huge amount of equipment (including aircraft, guns, tanks, trucks and radios) was destroyed or abandoned, either during the retreat or on the beaches. A New Zealand artillery officer recalled that his men fired their 25-pounder guns until 'the recuperators boiled and they seized up' and they 'drained the oil out of our trucks and ran them' to the same end.[12] With limited space, fitting men on the ships was more important than taking heavy equipment, but it would be sorely missed on Crete only a month later.

Most historians now regard the Greek campaign as a huge mistake by Churchill and his advisors. As Bernard Freyberg's son, Paul (who served in Greece), later wrote:

> There can be little doubt that the decision to break off pursuit of the beaten Italian army in Tripolitania [Libya] in favour of the Greek expedition was one of the biggest British military blunders of the Second World War. It diverted two well-found divisions, an armoured brigade, a number of RAF squadrons and a large administrative component from pursuing a limited and attainable objective in Africa in favour of an unlimited and unattainable one in Europe.[13]

But at the time, even critics recognised that there was a moral imperative of equal force to military reality. Three months after the defeat George Orwell wrote:

> No-one expected the Greek campaign to be anything but a disaster . . . on the other hand nearly everyone felt that it was our duty to intervene. It is generally recognised that as yet we can't fight the Germans on the continent of Europe but at the same time 'we couldn't let the Greeks down'.[14]

Left: A New Zealand soldier captured on Greece. [US National Archives: 242-GAP-159B-4]

1941

25 APRIL Hitler orders the invasion of Crete

New Zealand forces arrive on Crete

5th Brigade moves to Maleme

30 APRIL Freyberg appointed commander of Creforce

5 MAY

Student arrives in Athens

10 MAY

Heavy bombing begins at Maleme

10th Brigade established

15 MAY Fraser arrives in Egypt

Inglis arrives on Crete

RAF fighters withdrawn

20 MAY Germans ready for the invasion

3

BEST-LAID PLANS

A Kiwi soldier sailing to Crete in April 1941 might have repeated what Tasman wrote when he first sighted New Zealand almost 300 years before, seeing 'a large land, uplifted high'. Crete is dominated by a series of rugged limestone ranges running east to west along the entire 260 kilometre length of the island. These mountains fall steeply down to the south coast where, in 1941, there were only a few scattered fishing villages.

M̲ost of the 400,000 Cretans lived in the north, where fertile coastal flats were broken up by low hills and ridges. Fruit and vegetables were grown on small farms and everywhere stood groves of olive trees. The main towns on the coast were centres for commerce and fishing, with a large deep-water harbour at Suda Bay.

Inland were poor mountain villages, whose people lived mainly from sheep rearing, and the occasional stealing as well. A road ran along the north coast but, although the island is quite narrow (only 60 kilometres at its widest point), few routes went into the mountains.

With mainland Greece less than 100 kilometres away, Crete was difficult to defend from a determined invader. As both Freyberg and the Commander-in-Chief of the Mediterranean fleet, Admiral Cunningham, later said, Crete faced the wrong way. Its ports and small airfields in the north were vulnerable to attacks from Greece, while there were no good anchorages on the south coast. Anyone trying

Previous page: Soldiers evacuated from Greece arrive in Crete.
[ATL: DA-01611]

Below: A troopship unloading soldiers in Suda Bay. [War Museum, Canea]

Sea of Crete

N
W   E
S

Kasteli
Kisamou
Maleme
Galatas
Canea
Suda Bay
WHITE
MOUNTAINS
Kandanos
Retimo
Georgeoupolis
Heraklion
Knossos
Ay Roumeli
Sfakia
Crete
Sitia

Mediterranean Sea

0   50 km

Map: Key locations in the battle of Crete.

to defend the northern zone and bring in essential supplies by ship would face a difficult task.

The main base for the Royal Navy in the Mediterranean was Alexandria in Egypt so, once Italy entered the war, naval staff proposed a forward port at Suda Bay. After Mussolini attacked Greece, Britain sent anti-aircraft batteries to Crete. In November 1940 the New Zealand government was asked if some of its battalions in the Middle East could be despatched to help garrison the island but, because the brigades were scattered between Britain and Egypt, the idea was dropped. Although some British troops eventually arrived and began preparing defences, commanders of the garrison came and went, with five different senior officers between November 1940 and April 1941.

The last appointment was Major General Weston of the Royal Marines, who would play a significant role in the battle of Crete. A British historian who had served on Crete, Ian Stewart, described him as 'a regular officer, intelligent,

Below: New Zealand soldiers arrive off Crete.
[ATL: DA-01328]

Right: A trio of Kiwi engineers soon after their arrival in Crete.

[ATL: PAColl-4161-01-103]

courageous and capable of gaiety, but a man of moods, subject to fits of sudden despondency, which flawed his bearing and judgment'.[1] His initial defence plans were well thought out, however.

As the New Zealand troops evacuated from Greece arrived in Suda Bay they were greeted by a strange sight, a large British warship (the cruiser HMS *York*) beached on the edge of the harbour. It had been attacked by Italian motor boats filled with explosives, showing that one branch of the Italian forces could be as daring and courageous as Allied commandos. It was not the only wreck scattered around the harbour, but the others had been sunk in Luftwaffe air raids.

Weston dispersed the New Zealanders west of the port of Canea, along the beaches leading to the Maleme airfield (with the Australians kept around Suda Bay and two British battalions sent to Heraklion). For a few days the Kiwis believed they were taking a well-earned breather after the trials and tribulations of Greece, and that they would soon be sent back to Egypt. The men swam in the sea and sunbathed, and consumed oranges, eggs and vegetables obtained from local farmers, along with occasional bottles of wine. A private in the 23rd Battalion recorded in his diary:

> Weather fine. Am very happy and in the best of health . . . All we do is eat oranges and swim. Having a marvellous time. God! I'm as fit as a fiddle — a real box of birds! . . . This holiday we are having seems too damn good to last.[2]

He was right; the plans of politicians and generals would soon disrupt this brief idyll. The Germans knew that the conquest of Greece would not be complete until its many islands were occupied, and chief among them was the largest island, Crete. If the Allies stayed there, they could use its harbours and aerodromes to threaten Hitler's southern flank and the Romanian oilfields, while if Germany held Crete, it would possess a significant naval base and aircraft based there could bomb Alexandria and the Suez Canal. It might also be useful as a stepping stone for further assaults against Cyprus, Palestine and Egypt.

On 21 April 1941 these arguments were put to Hitler by an ambitious German general, Kurt Student. In the First World War he had been a fighter pilot, but in the interwar years he had become fascinated with the concept of using gliders and paratroops as a surprise strike force. Herman Goering, the head of the Luftwaffe, endorsed Student's ideas and an airborne division was established within the air force. The airborne forces had been successful during the attacks on Denmark, Norway, Belgium and the Netherlands in 1940 and now Student wanted to use them to take Crete.

Hitler had his doubts, correctly predicting that there would be many casualties. Also the invasions of Yugoslavia and Greece had put back the timetable for 'Operation Barbarossa' (the attack on the Soviet Union), and he did not want a risky Cretan adventure to cause further delay. Having made this qualification, he gave in to Goering's pressure and agreed to the airborne assault, to be codenamed 'Operation Merkur', after the Greco-Roman god with winged sandals, Mercury.

Below: Wavell and Freyberg (Egypt, 1940).

[ATL: Detail of DA-00645]

Churchill and his high command were soon aware of the German plans because, since 1940, British intelligence had been able to break the encoded signals sent by the Luftwaffe. (They later broke the German army and navy codes too.) This remarkable achievement was a closely held secret, and the information obtained, and the project itself, became known as 'Ultra'. It would be one of the key factors in the Allies' ultimate victory, as the Germans never realised that their top-secret signals were being read by their enemies.

Knowing the German plans confirmed Churchill's view that Crete could be held. The original reasons for defending Greece from attack could equally be applied to Crete, but for the embattled prime minister there was a more pressing rationale; the possibility that a success on Crete would make up for the fiasco in Greece. On 28 April he telegraphed General Wavell:

> It seems clear from our information that a heavy airborne attack by German troops and bombers will soon be made on Crete. Let me know what forces you have in the island and what your plans are. It ought to be a fine opportunity for killing the parachute troops.[3]

On the same day Major General Freyberg was waiting anxiously on a Greek beach for the Royal Navy to arrive and evacuate his division's 6th Brigade. They were taken off after midnight, with the commander and his staff the last to board, and arrived in Suda Bay a few hours later. Freyberg expected to move on to Egypt but fate, guided by the long arm of the British prime minister, intervened.

Early on 30 April the War Office in London, at Churchill's instigation, sent a signal to Wavell suggesting that Freyberg succeed Weston as the commander of the forces on Crete. Churchill had known Freyberg since the First World War and felt that this lion-hearted man of action was the right person to defend Crete. He would later send a personal cable to Freyberg, congratulating him on his 'vitally important command' and stating that he felt 'confident your fine troops will destroy parachutists man to man at close quarters'.[4]

Freyberg knew nothing of this when he and the other senior commanders on Crete were called to a conference at a villa west of Canea on 30 April. It was chaired by a tired-looking Wavell who had just flown in from Cairo. Freyberg wrote that Wavell took him aside and told him that he was to take command of the troops on Crete and prepare to defend the island against an attack 'in the next few days'. He was surprised and resisted the appointment, saying that his job was 'to get the New Zealand forces together again and get them retrained and re-equipped'. But Wavell said it was his 'duty to remain and take command' and so Freyberg, the loyal soldier, gave in.[5]

Wavell next told the assembled officers about the new command structure and the German plan of attack. He said the assault would be led by some 5,000 airborne troops, with a possible landing from the sea supported by tanks. The officers agreed that the obvious targets were the airfields at Heraklion and Maleme and the Canea-Suda Bay area.

The two generals then had further private discussions. Freyberg suggested that Crete be evacuated, but Wavell said there were simply not enough ships, for although more than 50,000 men had been taken off Greece only days earlier, a large number of ships had been sunk by the Luftwaffe. The second conversation was even more significant, as Wavell informed Freyberg that he would soon receive accurate and detailed information about the German invasion plans. The question remains — was Freyberg told that the source was Ultra or was he given a cover

Below: The view over Canea from Creforce headquarters as an air raid begins. [Sir John White]

story, namely, that Britain had a spy deep inside the German command in Athens?

In 1962, the year before he died, Bernard Freyberg told his son Paul that he knew that the intelligence was coming from Ultra but, because of the rules concerning the use of this top-secret material, he could not move his forces on Crete to the right locations to defeat the Germans. Because Ultra was still classified (and remained so for another decade), Paul was sworn to secrecy by his father. In the 1980s, however, he repeated his father's account publicly and it became an important theme in the biography he published in 1991.[6]

It is true that in the early days of Ultra, in order to ensure that the Germans would not realise that their codes had been broken, British commanders in the know were forbidden to take any actions that could lead to German suspicions. If Ultra information was to be acted on, further supporting evidence was required. For example, when the Italian fleet was battered by their British counterpart off Cape Matapan in March 1941, Admiral Cunningham already knew from Ultra intercepts that it would be there. However, he first sent over a flying boat so the Italians would think they had been located by aerial reconnaissance.

When Paul Freyberg repeated his father's account, some old colleagues believed it but others did not.[7] The doubters could not accept that the general they knew would not have found a way around the Ultra rules, if following them meant losing a battle. Some pointed out that in fact various troop dispositions were changed on Crete before the fighting began. Others, noting that Freyberg was infamous for not being able to keep a secret,[8] felt that it was unlikely he was told about Ultra at the time, even if he learnt about it later in the war or after 1945.

Some documents, however, suggest Freyberg may have been told about Ultra,[9] and Churchill certainly was willing to send the actual texts of decrypted signals to the general on Crete, rather than information filtered through intelligence analysis. (He dropped this proposal when his advisors warned it might lead to the Germans learning about Ultra.)

The debate remains, but whether or not Freyberg knew about Ultra while on Crete, there is no doubt he treated the intelligence he received very seriously. Over the weeks before the battle a steady stream of information arrived. It was sent in code to the radio station at RAF headquarters on Crete where a liaison officer decoded it and took it to Freyberg. Fortunately he had a good memory, because the signals were burnt immediately after he had read them.

Following the meeting with Wavell on 30 April, Freyberg's first action was to set up a headquarters for Creforce, as his command was named. It was located in a quarry on the hill above Canea, looking west along the coast towards Maleme over 20 kilometres away. Weston, perhaps piqued at losing his position, had taken his men with him back to the Suda Bay defences, so Freyberg had to set up a staff from scratch. Geoffrey Cox wrote that Weston's action 'rankled in his [Freyberg's] mind in later years' and he would often refer to it when Crete was discussed.[10]

The next day, having assessed the forces available to defend the island, Freyberg sent strongly worded telegrams to Wavell and Peter Fraser. He told Wavell that 'the forces at my disposal are totally inadequate to meet the attack envisaged' and demanded further assistance, especially from the RAF and Royal Navy.[11] More supplies and naval support were promised but, because of pressures elsewhere, sending additional fighter aircraft to supplement the meagre number already on Crete would be difficult.

Freyberg repeated the problems to the New Zealand prime minister, emphasising 'the grave situation in which the bulk of the Division is placed' and asking him to put pressure on the British government. Fraser's immediate response was a telegram to Churchill, stating 'that our troops should either be supplied with sufficient means to defend the island, or that the decision to hold Crete at all costs should be reviewed'.[12] Worried that the debacle in Greece might be repeated on Crete, Fraser decided that he had to be closer to the action and, as he was already going back to London, immediately set off for Cairo. His presence would ultimately save a number of Kiwis from prisoner-of-war camps.

Having made his protests, Freyberg set about organising his forces. He had some 30,000 British, Australian and New Zealand troops and 10,000 Greeks, but not all of them were fighting men. A number of the evacuees from the mainland were members of supporting units, including labourers from Palestine and Cyprus. There were also Greek civilian evacuees, notably the royal family, politicians and civil servants. All of them had to fed and housed, which put further pressure on the supply route through Suda Bay, where air raids were increasing.

Freyberg soon got rid of some of the surplus men and civilians. He also sent the British, Australian and New Zealand nurses, who had performed well in Greece, back to Egypt. They were furious as they had withstood the strafing and bombing equally with the men, but the general later said: 'I could not agree to women being mixed up in the shambles that was about to commence.'[13] In any event, their ship received unwelcome attention from the Luftwaffe before it reached safer waters.

Most of the soldiers who landed on Crete from Greece had arrived with little but their personal weapons and the clothes on their backs. Haddon Donald, a junior officer in the 22nd Battalion, recalled their plight:

Below: New Zealand nurses awaiting evacuation from Crete.

[P. Ryan/Filer collection]

We were fairly short of ammunition and we had no picks and shovels, nearly all our gear had been tossed overboard because there wasn't much room on the ship coming over, we had our weapons alright, but nothing much else . . . eventually a few spades and shovels and picks came through and we shared these around and [with] bayonets and tin hats and whatever other local tools we could find, we dug some dirt trenches.[14]

Freyberg was surprised when he went round the troops and saw that 'men had

Left: Soldiers, nurses and civilians in a Cretan village. [P. Ryan/Filer collection]

Above, left & right:
Many New Zealand
soldiers arrived on
Crete with little other
than their personal
equipment.
[P. Harwood/P. Ryan/Filer
collection]

no arms or equipment, and no plates, knives, forks or spoons and they ate and drank from bully beef or cigarette tins'.[15] He was even more concerned, however, about the shortages in tanks, artillery and trucks, along with essential parts for mortars and machine guns. A detailed wish list was sent to Wavell and some tanks, guns, rifles and additional troops arrived before the battle commenced.

From Egypt 2NZEF headquarters despatched two army bands, the Kiwi Concert Party and the official war artist, Peter McIntyre. They were pleased to be sailing on a Dutch freighter named *Nieuw Zeeland*, along with a British tank commander, Roy Farran, who would play a significant part in the coming conflict.

One of worst shortages was in communications equipment, with many radios having been dumped on the beaches in Greece. Some RAF gear was shared around and telephone cables were laid between key headquarters. They were easily damaged by bombing, however, and once the invasion occurred, the paratroopers cut any lines they found. Also, as historian Matthew Wright has noted, the radios available on Crete were vulnerable to 'peculiar atmospheric conditions and lack of a suitable power supply'.[16]

There is no doubt that additional radios would have helped the Allied commanders, as communications during the battle were often reduced to the oldest form possible, the runner. Carrying messages on foot, particularly under aerial bombardment, was far more vulnerable than speaking into a microphone. Geoffrey Cox would later write:

> A hundred Mark II wireless sets could have saved Crete. Indeed, half a dozen of them — enough to maintain contact around the airfield at Maleme, might have tipped the scales.[17]

In comparison to the desperate need for equipment, Freyberg felt he could cope with the numbers of fighting men available to him, although it was impossible to cover every place where the Germans could land. He allocated his troops primarily to defend Suda Bay and other northern ports, the airfields at Maleme, Retimo and Heraklion, and potential sites for sea landings.

His operation instruction issued on 4 May laid out the order of battle, with four main sectors and commanders. Heraklion was to be defended by the British 14th Infantry Brigade and an Australian battalion, under the command of Brigadier Chappel. In the centre, covering both Retimo and Georgeoupolis, was Brigadier Vasey's 19th Australian Brigade. Weston continued to lead the British troops, marines and gunners at Suda Bay, while Brigadier Puttick was now in command of the New Zealand Division in the nearby Maleme sector. But Suda Bay was some 50 kilometres from Retimo and Heraklion another 60 kilometres further east so, once the battle began these sectors, in effect, had to fight it out by themselves.

Within each brigade were battalions varying in strength and experience. Some had a full complement, while others had been badly weakened by the loss of men in Greece. Certain battalions were given a static role, in particular, defending an airfield, while others had to be ready to counter-attack the invaders and push them off any foothold they gained. Although Antony Beevor has implied that Freyberg did not emphasise the importance of vigorous counter-attack, the orders that went out to the various units clearly indicate the reverse.[18]

Each sector included one or more Greek regiments, which historian and Crete veteran Dan Davin described as 'for the most part untrained, ill-equipped and unorganised' and 'armed with five different types of rifle and an average of less than 20 rounds of ammunition per man'.[19] Yet the Greeks would fight tenaciously and the western port of Kastelli Kisamou was defended solely by a Greek regiment (assisted by some New Zealand instructors) and the local police force. The Cretan populace, too, would bring out their hidden weapons and join in the struggle.

Below: A signaller at New Zealand divisional headquarters.
[ATL: DA-13275]

Freyberg ensured that the small numbers of anti-aircraft and field guns (including old French weapons and Italian guns without sights) were shared among the sectors and that tanks were sent to each airfield. They were dug in and camouflaged so they could suddenly appear to lead the counter-attacks after the Germans had landed.

New Zealand's 5th Brigade under Brigadier Hargest was given the key role of defending Maleme airfield and the eastern approaches to it. He placed his strongest unit, the 22nd Battalion, around the airfield and on Kavzakia Hill, the low hill which overlooked it, which was known to the troops as 'Point 107' because that was its height in metres. The battalion was commanded by Lieutenant Colonel Leslie Andrew, a Regular officer who

was well known as a strict disciplinarian, and for winning the Victoria Cross in the First World War. Stewart pointedly described Andrew as a man whose 'professional views were wholly orthodox. Now his orders were to fight a battle of static defence, maintaining the protection of the airfield "at all cost". It was task for which his qualities seemed to suit him perfectly.'[20]

To the east of 22nd Battalion's positions were two other New Zealand battalions, with the 23rd (which was given the main counter-attack role) near the coast and the 21st on the hills next to the village of Kondomari. The latter battalion was at less than half strength having lost many of its men in Greece during and after the disastrous action in the Pinios Gorge. They were unexpectedly reinforced in early May when some of their soldiers, along with Lieutenant Colonel Macky, arrived on Crete following an adventurous escape across the Greek islands. Macky, who was suffering from dysentery, was sent to hospital and then back home, his overseas service at an end. During the battle the battalion would be commanded by Lieutenant Colonel Allen, a pre-war MP.

Further east again, along the coast road, was an engineer detachment fighting as infantry and beyond them around the township of Platanias was the 28th (Maori) Battalion. Most of this battalion had seen little action on Greece and were still awaiting their first real battle. To the south a Field Punishment Centre had been set up to hold the bad boys of the division, who would soon direct their aggression at the Germans. Hargest meanwhile established his headquarters in a farmhouse on the hill above Platanias which gave him good views over his sector but was too far away from the main target, the airfield, if communications failed.

A bigger problem for 5th Brigade lay to the west of the airfield and Point 107. There were no spare soldiers to put in the nearby Tavronitis River valley or on the open ground beyond, where airborne troops could land unopposed and form up to advance on the airfield. Freyberg and Puttick considered moving the Greek regiment from Kastelli Kisamou but in the end decided to leave it there, where it would in fact be needed.

East of 5th Brigade and nearer to Canea, a line of hills and ridges centred on the village of Galatas were allocated to a scratch infantry unit made up of New Zealand gunners and drivers evacuated from Greece (which became the 'Composite Battalion'). As the strategic importance of this area was recognised, the unit was strengthened and renamed 10th Brigade. Howard Kippenberger took command, while his own battalion, the 20th, joined the brigade, along with two Greek regiments. He inherited an unfortunate decision to place one of the regiments in an isolated location overlooking the prison in the valley below Galatas, a position he complained was 'murder'. The blunt reply was that 'in war murder sometimes has to be done'.[21]

Around Canea and Suda Bay were some British units and New Zealand's 4th Brigade, now down to two battalions. Its role was to be the reserve for Creforce and Brigadier Lindsay Inglis was brought across from Egypt to take command. He was one of the distinctive characters of the New Zealand Division, although not always a pleasant one. Stewart's description was apt:

As a soldier there still clung to him something of the attitudes that he had learnt in his civilian profession as a lawyer. Highly intelligent, quick-thinking and volatile in argument, he was also pugnacious and opinionated, adept at proving to his own satisfaction that any failure with which he might be associated could not relate to any inadequacy of his own. It is a skill that colleagues seldom find endearing.[22]

Inglis was also fond of a drink, so much so that he was nicknamed 'Whisky Bill', although his tipple did not seem to affect his military judgement.

Having re-organised his command and commanders, Freyberg then toured the various sectors, inspecting the defences and addressing the officers and men. He outlined how the assault was expected to unfold and emphasised that Crete must be held. Understandably, he was more positive and sanguine than perhaps he felt, as Davin recalled:

Above: Andrew, Hargest and Freyberg (Egypt, 1941).
[ATL: DA-13918]

Map: New Zealand positions in the Maleme sector.

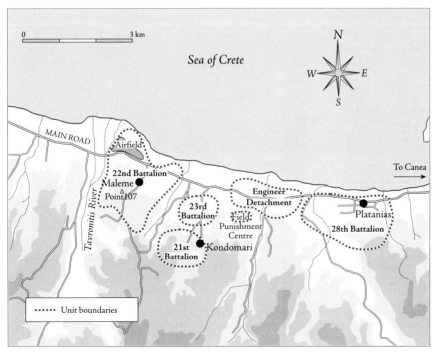

Above: Officers of the 20th Battalion have their first meal on Crete. Howard Kippenberger is in the centre and Charles Upham on the far right.
[ATL: DA-10561]

Below: Lindsay Inglis (Egypt, 1941).
[ATL: DA-01514]

I can remember him coming to our battalion [the 23rd] which was very close to Maleme airfield twice. The first time he pepped us up with all sorts of spiel about what we would do to the Germans . . . and the second time he did the same thing, but there was a different type of note in his voice and I think by that time he knew how tremendous the odds were against us.[23]

As the Luftwaffe stepped up their air raids, it became increasingly difficult for Freyberg to get around the troops. His aide-de-camp Jack Griffiths (a pre-war All Black captain) later said:

We would be on the road endeavouring to get over as much of the island as possible. It did reach a stage where it was virtually impossible to move by day, there were continual air attacks and strafing . . . which made communications very, very difficult. In fact, it was almost non-existent once the battle started.[24]

At the same time as Freyberg and his commanders were preparing their defences, General Student and his staff were planning the attack. They had arrived in Athens in early May and set themselves up in the Hotel Grand Bretagne (where the Greek high command and British military mission had previously been based). Over the next two weeks Student's paratroops assembled at the airfields of southern Greece, while an army division, the Bavarians and Austrians of the 5th Mountain Division, led by Major General Ringel, also joined the operation. Other army units in Greece were available, adding up to a total force of over 22,000 men.

The invasion plan would be described today as a strategy of 'shock and awe', where a swift, violent, surprise attack so confuses and demoralises the defenders that their resistance is minimal. Glider-borne troops were to strike at crucial targets near Maleme and Suda Bay, while the paratroopers were to land directly on and around the three airfields, and south of Canea. Instead of concentrating on one target, Student felt confident enough to invade all four defence sectors on the first day. This was a dangerous dispersal of his airborne forces but he believed that the key points would be seized. Later that day, or the next one, transport planes would fly in the 5th Mountain Division, and more troops, supplies and guns were to reach Crete on the second day of the invasion on two flotillas of light ships.

It was a bold plan with a fatal flaw: the failure of German intelligence about all aspects of the defence of Crete. Freyberg had sensibly insisted that his commanders ensure that their positions were well camouflaged and that their men would not fire unnecessarily at enemy aircraft. So although the Germans had studied the maps and sent reconnaissance flights over the island, they had not located the hidden guns and tanks or seen the infantry lying beneath the ubiquitous olive trees. They believed that most of the Allied troops evacuated from Greece had gone back to Egypt and that there were only 5,000 British soldiers on the island. In addition, they did not read the terrain accurately and planned to drop gliders and paratroopers in hazardous areas. As Freyberg himself later wrote:

> . . . although their plan was well made and relentlessly carried out, they planned it in the only possible way to defeat their own troops. The Germans made every mistake except attacking on a narrow front. How near they came to defeat one will never know.[25]

Left: A well in the Prison Valley.
[ATL: DA-03727]

The most outlandish intelligence blunder was the belief that the people of Crete would welcome the German invasion. Perhaps Student's staff had been told about the Cretan dislike of the Athens dictatorship and the king and, therefore, had assumed that the paratroopers would be welcomed as liberators. They would get a terrible shock when the Cretans rose to defend their homeland.

The attack was originally planned for 15 May, but had to be put back to the 17th and then to the 20th. Assembling all the men and aircraft was a complex operation and there were supply bottlenecks, particularly with aviation fuel. When the bridge over the Corinth Canal had been destroyed on 26 April, the debris had blocked the waterway, and ships bringing fuel from Italy were unable to use it. The canal was not cleared until 17 May and all the supplies did not reach the airfields until the night before the invasion.

As the assault plans firmed up they were transmitted to the relevant headquarters and, unbeknown to the Germans, intercepted by British listening posts. After decoding via Ultra, summaries were prepared and sent to Crete directly or through Middle East Command. Freyberg received a steady stream of information, not all of which was helpful. Intelligence analysts overestimated the size of the invading force, which grew like Topsy. On 13 May Freyberg was told it would 'consist of some 30 to 35,000 men, of which some 12,000 will be the parachute landing contingent and 10,000 will be transported by sea'.[26] This was a gross exaggeration of the actual numbers in the seaborne element. Beevor has written that Freyberg 'lacked the analytical intellect and the scepticism necessary to identify inconsistencies' with earlier information,[27] but the detailed summaries he had received on 6 and 7 May had provided no figures at all for the size of the seaborne force.

Below: Freyberg addressing a group of officers on Crete.
[Australian War Memorial: 069892]

The Ultra information was more accurate about the huge air armada available for the attack. There were up to 600 transport planes (mainly the Junkers 52, the Luftwaffe's workhorse) to carry the paratroopers and supplies, along with 70 gliders. This fleet of aircraft, 'the largest ever seen',[28] steadily arrived at the Greek airfields. Providing fighter and bomber support was the VIII Air Corps, with some 570 planes, under the command of General Freiherr von Richthofen (a cousin of the 'Red Baron' of First World War fame). With so many aircraft spread around more than 15 airfields, coordinating all the attacks would prove a difficult operation.

Opposing this massive force were a few obsolete British fighters based on Crete, supplemented by the battered RAF squadrons which had flown in from Greece. Some additional Hurricanes arrived from Egypt, but there were usually less than a dozen serviceable fighters available to counter the

Luftwaffe's raids at any one time. In the weeks leading up to the invasion the RAF shot down a number of German aircraft, but by 19 May only seven British fighters were left, so it was decided to send them back to Egypt rather than have them wiped out during the invasion. However, at the RAF's insistence, no substantial obstructions were put on the airfields to prevent the enemy using them. As Freyberg later stated:

> . . . the Air Officer Commanding made it clear that none of the three aerodromes should be permanently obstructed. Although the few remaining fighters were ordered to Egypt before the battle, the intention was that the fighters should return as soon as possible and make use of the aerodromes. In point of fact Heraklion was so used.[29]

Above: German troops in Athens. [P. Harwood/Filer collection]

Below: Paratroopers on a Greek airfield.
[ATL: DA-11989]

With so little opposition, the Luftwaffe was able to carry out a series of bombing raids, which got steadily heavier as the invasion date approached. Consequently, it became more difficult to bring in supplies through Suda Bay and exposed defences, like the anti-aircraft guns around Maleme airfield, were easily destroyed. But for the men hiding in

FALLSCHIRMJAGER

The paratroopers (*Fallschirmjager*) formed one of the elite forces of the German armed services in the Second World War. They were less imbued with Nazi ideology than some of the other elites (such as the *Waffen SS*), but their younger members had grown up in the Hitler Youth and believed in Germany's military and cultural superiority and the need to right the 'wrongs' of the peace settlement at the end of the First World War. Some of the older officers and non-commissioned officers (NCO's) came from Prussian families with long military traditions (including a number opposed to the Nazis). Most paratroopers though were fit young men who had volunteered to do something different and more adventurous than standard German military service.

A German paratrooper. [ATL: DA-12631]

Each volunteer had to do at least six successful jumps during training to receive the distinctive parachutist's badge. In action, they usually jumped from a Junkers 52 aircraft, which carried about a dozen paratroopers and four equipment containers. They leapt from a low height, around 100 metres, and the parachutes were not fully open until the men were halfway down. It would take 20 to 30 seconds to reach the ground.

Unfortunately, the German parachute harness was not a good design. It was attached to the chute by a single strap in the centre of the back, which meant the wearer had little control over the direction of descent. Because of this flaw, some of the men landing on Crete were injured on rocky ground or drowned along the coast.

Another problem was that the German paratrooper of 1941 jumped carrying only a pistol and a dagger, although some men also had sub-machine guns and grenades. Their rifles and heavier weapons were in the containers dropped with them but, if they could not reach this equipment, they were very vulnerable to counter-attack. Many paratroopers were killed on Crete because they had only short-range weapons to defend themselves.

Against this, paratroopers were taught to show a high level of personal initiative, aggression and flexibility. The full meaning of their unit's operation was explained to them, so that if their commanders became casualties, they could take over. (This was common practice throughout the German armed forces, and one of the reasons for their great success in the early years of the Second World War.)

Glider-borne assault units were often dropped in advance of the paratroopers, to seize or eliminate key targets. These airborne troops had an even more dangerous existence than their parachuting comrades, as many gliders crashed on takeoff or landing and they were easily hit by ground fire. Despite high casualties, however, the glider troops played an important role in the battle of Crete.

Crete was the last mass attack by the *Fallschirmjager*, although paratroop drops did occur during operations later in the war. However, most of the airborne divisions were turned into motorised infantry forces and served alongside the German army in all theatres of conflict. As elite units, they suffered horrendous casualties, with more than 60,000 killed or missing in action before the German surrender in May 1945.[30]

FALLSCHIRMJAGER

trenches beneath the olive trees, the air attacks were more frightening than deadly. When the 22nd Battalion was plastered with bombs the day before the invasion, the casualties were low, with only one man killed and two wounded (although, around the same time, one man in Haddon Donald's platoon appeared to die 'of fright or despair').[31]

However, the constant raids had a numbing effect on the commanders and their staff who had to make decisions and move around. Howard Kippenberger noted at the time that 'total air superiority against one induces feelings of inferiority and pessimism that are very hard to combat'[32] and a senior staff officer, Bill Gentry, later wrote that:

> The constant drone of planes flying over the tree tops spraying the area with M.G. [machine guns] was very monotonous & on me at least induced great sleepiness. The effect was that you could not move about, no walkers or runner & no cars as they were sitting shots. The telephone lines were always bombed out & communication was very difficult . . . night was the time when everything had to be done.[33]

It now seems likely that the air attacks had a profound effect on one key commander, Brigadier Hargest, bringing on another bout of the shell shock he had suffered since the First World War and the lethargy and confusion that went with it. Initially he had appeared self-assured and resilient, writing in a letter on 10 May: 'I know I am trusted & I know that in a crisis my judgement is sound & my instincts right & that mostly I am without personal fear.'[34] Yet nine days later, when Geoffrey Cox visited him on the eve of battle, that confidence had wilted. As they looked out across the sea to where the airborne assault force would soon appear, Hargest said:

> I don't know what lies ahead. I only know that it produces in me a sensation I never knew in the last war. It is not fear. It is something quite different, something which I can only describe as dread.[35]

Below: Ships on fire in Suda Bay after an air raid.
[ATL: DA-13172]

1941
19 MAY
MIDNIGHT
20 MAY

First German aircraft take off in Greece

6 A.M.   Heavy bombing on Crete
Gliders and paratroopers land on Crete
Germans on the Tavronitis River
Germans capture the hospital
Germans capture Pink Hill

NOON

Tank counter-attack at Maleme
6 P.M.   Hargest agrees to withdrawal from
Point 107

Counter-attack in the Prison Valley

First withdrawal from Point 107

20 MAY
MIDNIGHT
21 MAY   22 Battalion withdraws from Maleme

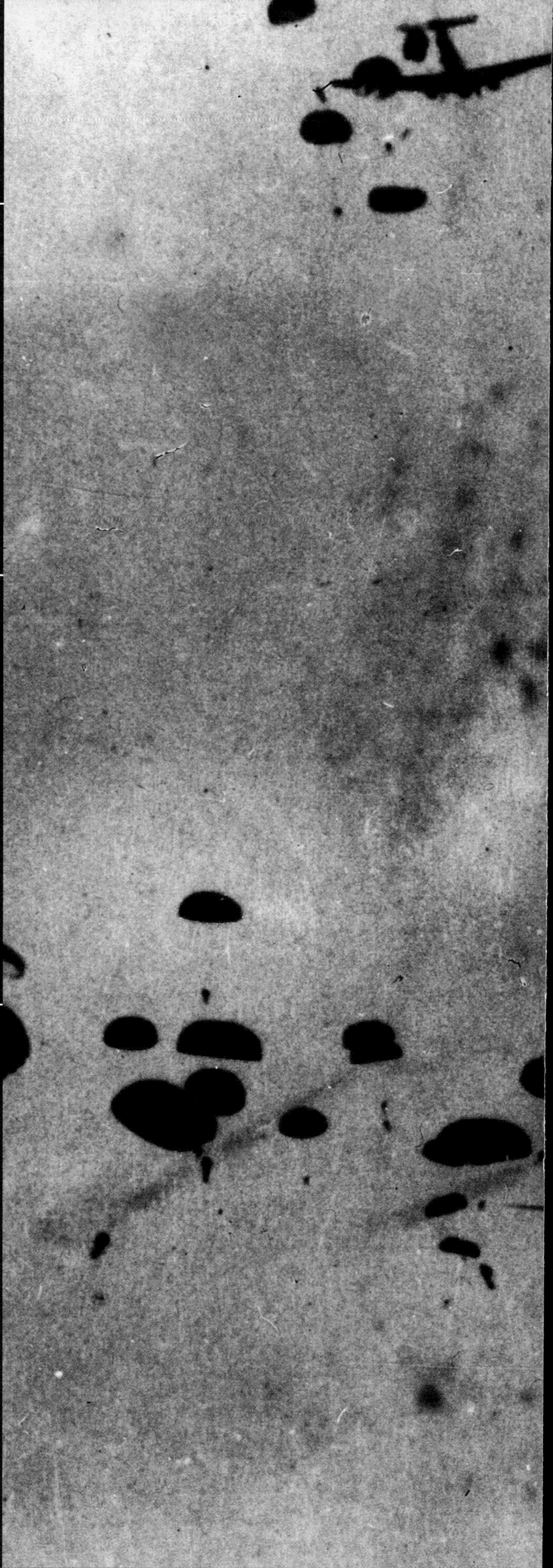

4

DAY ONE: CANEA, MALEME AND GALATAS

The battle for Crete began in the early hours of Tuesday 20 May 1941, but not on the island where most civilians and soldiers were still sleeping in their beds or resting under the olive trees. The first act took place on the airfields of mainland Greece as fighters and bombers were armed, transport planes were loaded, mechanics pumped fuel and paratroopers checked their kit.

Before the day dawned the advance formations, the gliders and their tow-planes, took off and turned to the south. In an inauspicious beginning, the rope on the glider carrying the commander of the Parachute Division snapped over the island of Aegina and it plummeted to the ground, killing all on board.

Soon the fighters, bombers and troop carriers were ascending into the pale dawn light. Most of the paratroopers were deep in thought, knowing that this day could be their last. Captain (Baron) von der Heydte of the 3rd Parachute Regiment recalled the moment:

> Except for the crew, not one of the thirteen men seated in the plane uttered a word. Everyone was preoccupied with his own thoughts. When there is no going back, most men experience a strange sinking feeling, as if their stomachs had remained on the ground.[1]

Previous page: The aerial invasion of Crete.
[ATL: DA-11980]

Below: German paratroopers pose outside their aircraft before flying to Crete.
[Filer collection]

First over Crete were the war planes, which carried out an intense attack on key targets along the north coast. A woman who lived in Canea said that even the animals sensed the danger, with 'the dogs and the pigeons moaning and screeching with fear'.[2] At Maleme airfield the bombing and strafing went on for 90 minutes, with around 3,000 bombs being dropped, blasting away much of the vegetation camouflaging the defences. The soldiers of the 22nd Battalion huddled in their trenches, their minds and bodies numbed by violent shock waves, choking dust and smoke, and thunderous noise. A Kiwi soldier later recorded the experience in his diary:

> One continuous scream and crash of bombs. All bleeding at ears and mouth from concussion; trench walls shaking and crumbling in; couldn't see next man for dust and cordite.[3]

Platoon commander Haddon Donald remembered being 'actually concussed for a short while and I had to get a shake on the shoulder to bring me round'.[4] But before the smoke had cleared the next stage of the attack was underway, with gliders sweeping in eerily across the sea and paratroopers falling from the sky.

The time was around 8 a.m. and Freyberg was eating his breakfast at Creforce headquarters outside Canea. Looking up to see the gliders and parachutes in the distance, he glanced at his watch and muttered 'dead on time', before resuming his meal. An English officer wrote that 'his attitude was that he had already made all the necessary dispositions on the basis of his information, and there was now nothing more for him to do except leave his subordinates to fight the battle'.[5]

Suddenly the fight came close to Creforce headquarters as gliders soared past to land members of the Storm Regiment less than a kilometre away. Their target, however, was the anti-aircraft guns (some of which were dummies) protecting Canea and Suda Bay, not the headquarters. Grim-faced British troops moved up the hill to engage the enemy, shooting up their aircraft and killing or capturing some, but not all, of the assault troops. A Cretan later saw in one wrecked glider, '10–12 blond god-like youngsters, no more than 18–20 years old, lying dead in a row'.[6]

Other airborne troops landed south of Canea and in the valley below Galatas. The sky was soon full of planes and parachutes, as a New Zealand officer vividly described:

> Low-flying Dorniers swept us with a hail of lead, Stukas dive-bombed . . . gliders slid over them where the mammoth troop carriers nosed in, and then right up to the ceiling of the sky whirled the ever-watchful Messerschmitts. The Condors swerved astride the valley road and suddenly the sky was raining falling petals, tiers of planes simultaneously disgorging lines of black parachutes . . . interspersed with these were white sheets dropping stores, yellow with medical supplies and green with mortars.[7]

The sudden descent of the paratroopers was a frightening and awe-inspiring sight for the soldiers defending Crete. Many Kiwis had never seen a parachutist before,

Below left: Freyberg and his aide-de-camp, Jack Griffith, watching the invasion on 20 May 1941. [Sir John White]

Below right: Dead assault troops lie beside their glider.
[ATL: DA-01156]

Right: Paratroopers
dropping over Crete.

[P. Harwood/Filer collection]

let alone hundreds of armed men leaping from the transport planes. For a few
seconds the soldiers on the ground gaped, before they raised their rifles and began
to fire. For good shots it was too easy, and the common remark afterwards was that
it was 'just like duck shooting'. Charles Bennett of the Maori Battalion later said:

> It was no trouble at all for blokes to shoot them down and in some cases they
> were being shot down like game birds . . . you can always tell when you've
> shot a parachutist because as he jumps out of his aircraft he gets his blood
> circulation going by using his legs almost as if he's cycling and then when he
> had a shot in him, his legs just get taut, of course, and you know you can now
> turn your rifle on the next one.[8]

For the Germans in the air, dropping over these well-defended positions was a
terrifying experience. One paratrooper who survived, recalled that his parachute
had scarcely opened when bullets began spitting past from all directions: 'It had felt
so splendid just before to jump in sunlight over such wonderful countryside, but my
feelings suddenly changed. All I could do was to pull my head in and cover my face
with my arms.'[9]

Later, some captured parachutists would complain that it was 'unsporting' to
shoot at them while they were still in the sky but, as Davin would eloquently write,
'each man dangling carried a death, his own if not another's'.[10]

Even as they landed on the ground, the paratroopers remained vulnerable. Some found themselves completely alone, without a comrade in sight. They all had to get out of their harnesses and locate their weapons containers, but many were immediately despatched by Kiwis close by. The experience of the 23rd Battalion east of Maleme was typical. After watching the first wave of the invasion descend around the airfield, the battalion commander, Lieutenant Colonel Leckie, sent some platoons out to 'clean up' the Germans who had landed beyond his defence perimeter. The isolated paratroopers were easy targets and one platoon, led by Second Lieutenant 'Sandy' Thomas, killed 29 enemy and captured three, for the loss of only two of its men. When Thomas got back to the battalion he found that hundreds of paratroopers, who had been foolishly dropped directly over it, had been slaughtered. Leckie had killed five falling right on his headquarters and his adjutant had shot two without getting up from his desk.

Thomas wrote that the 'whole area was an unforgettable sight, with parachutes of all colours draped from practically every tree. Some of them still had their soldiers held in harness, swinging to and fro from the branches.' Meanwhile, Davin (the battalion's intelligence officer) noted the 'savage elation' he and his men felt after killing the enemy.[11]

Similar deeds were carried out near by, where the division's law-breakers had been released from the Field Punishment Centre and given weapons. Along with the military police (including Sergeant Clive Hulme, who would win the Victoria Cross for his actions on Crete), they stalked and killed over 100 paratroopers who landed near the prison, as well as protecting a troop of Kiwi gunners. To their west the members of 21st Battalion made up for their failure on Greece by eliminating all the Germans who had dropped in their zone. They were assisted by the Cretans from the village of Kondomari, who were soon exchanging their old guns, axes and knives for modern German weapons.

Many of the paratroopers could not find or reach their weapons containers. When one group eventually crept up to a container they realised it held only the battalion signal equipment, which a non-commissioned officer smashed 'out of frustration'.[12]

Left: New Zealand soldiers in a parachute-draped olive grove. [M. Clark/Filer collection]

Far left: A dead paratrooper. [N.E. Andrews/ Filer collection]

Above: Paratroopers fall over New Zealand positions at Galatas.

[ATL: DA-11022]

Meanwhile, all across the battle zone, the Kiwis and Cretans were opening containers, and also examining the clothes and equipment of dead or captured paratroopers. Corporal Jeff Spence of the 19th Battalion crawled towards a dead German 'to get his Luger and hand grenades . . . and a Leica camera as well'.[13] Charles Upham with the 20th Battalion was fascinated by all the zips on the heavy German jumpsuits, as zips on clothes were virtually unheard of in pre-war New Zealand. And Captain Hanton of the 22nd Battalion noted that:

> . . . during the lulls the men grabbed any German stores that landed near them. There were canisters of gear, food, motor cycles and even warm coffee from Hun flasks. The detailed organisation of the force amazed us at the time; we had not realised that so much care could be taken to win a battle.[14]

The problem for the German commanders, however, was they were losing the battle, not winning it. In fact many senior officers had been killed, wounded or captured, and their juniors had been forced to take command. It was fortunate that General Student had been forbidden to land with the assault force, or he, too, would likely have been a casualty. In most parts of the New Zealand sector the first wave of the invasion had been a costly failure for the Germans, but in two places, near Maleme airfield and south of Galatas, small footholds had been gained. These would prove crucial as the tide of battle turned.

When the gliders swooped in over the airfield (looking like 'big sharks' according

Previous page: Peter McIntyre, *Parachutists landing on Galatas.*

[Archives New Zealand: AAAC 898 NCWA 16]

Left: Peter McIntyre, *5th Brigade's Forward Dressing Station near Maleme.* The New Zealand medical staff are helping both wounded Kiwis and German prisoners. [Archives New Zealand: AAAC 898 NCWA 81]

Above: Peter McIntyre, *Crashed German glider.*

[Archives New Zealand: AAAC 898 NCWA 75]

These two pages feature rarely seen stills from the only known colour film shot in Greece and Crete. Reproduced with permission of J. Irwin.

Refugees in Greece.

Soldiers evacuated from Greece.

A body wash on Crete.

Relaxing at a Cretan beach.

Greek soldiers share a drink with Cretan civilians.

Kiwis playing cards.

Soldiers in a village street.

Kiwis manning a trench.

Taking cover in a trench.

German planes over Crete.

Soldiers on a warship leaving Crete.

Navy anti-aircraft gunners.

Above: Peter McIntyre, *Bombing of 7th General Hospital.*

[Archives New Zealand: AAAC 898 NCWA 76]

Above: Peter McIntyre, *General Hospital Crete*. German paratroopers landed on the military hospital soon after it was bombed. [Archives New Zealand: AAAC 898 NCWA 301]

Next page: Peter McIntyre, *The barge from Crete*. Some soldiers who were not evacuated from Crete found an abandoned landing craft and used it to escape to Egypt. [Archives New Zealand: AAAC 898 NCWA 14]

to one New Zealander), their targets were Point 107 and the Tavronitis river valley. The men who landed on the slopes of the hill were quickly despatched by the Kiwis, but the troops who skidded into the dry river valley were soon in action. They took control of the bridge over the river and although the bed was too hard to dig in (one of the reasons Freyberg and Puttick had decided not to put men there), they were able to find shelter under the banks and fire on the Kiwis above.

At the same time more than one thousand paratroopers, who had dropped around the undefended villages or on open ground further west, were regrouping, finding their weapons containers, and moving up to join the glider troops.

Lieutenant Colonel Andrew was commanding the 22nd Battalion from a trench on the south slope of Point 107. He knew the enemy had landed, but from his position he could not see his forward companies which were dug in around the airfield (C Company) and above the river bed (D Company). In any event, the bombing and strafing had forced him to keep under cover, and he had been wounded slightly when a bomb splinter struck his temple. According to the battalion history, 'a man nearby heard the angry Colonel exclaim: "We'll go out and get these b—s when the bombing stops."'[15]

But it was the Germans who took the early initiative. They attacked towards the airfield and penetrated the New Zealand defences, overrunning one platoon by the middle of the day. The administration camp for the airfield just east of the bridge was also taken and most of the British personnel there were captured. In the first of a number of similar occasions on Crete, the Germans used their prisoners as a screen as they advanced on the defenders' positions. This breach of the rules of war did not succeed, as Haddon Donald later described:

> Down towards the Tavronitis bridge there was a concentration of British troops, air force personnel and some marines . . . about midday or maybe in the early afternoon, we saw a number of [them] who had been rounded up by the Germans coming round the hillside towards us, spread out with the Germans following behind with machine guns trained on them, and obviously the Germans were using this as a device to try and make us surrender. As they came closer we called out to the British troops to lie down, which they did, and we shot up the Germans that were approaching behind them. They then came and joined us and were quite a welcome reinforcement.[16]

Despite this success, the German pressure around the hill and the airfield continued and other forward posts were gradually overrun. It was difficult for Lieutenant Colonel Andrew to know exactly what was happening, as his telephone lines had been cut early on and radio links with brigade headquarters and the other battalions were intermittent. The fog of war had descended and he was reduced to using runners to maintain contact with his companies. One of his men would note that Andrew and his second-in-command, 'showed signs of strain during the day, and I put this down to lack of news and information concerning their own troops and the position in general'.[17]

Some fifteen kilometres further east the Germans were consolidating their second foothold, in the Prison Valley below the village of Galatas. Three battalions of paratroopers (some 1,600 men) had dropped in the morning on or around Galatas, while an engineer battalion landed near Lake Aghya to the south-west (with many of the men who unluckily fell into the lake being drowned). As at Maleme, the invaders who dropped directly over the New Zealand positions were slaughtered, with more than 150 paratroopers being killed or captured in the 19th Battalion's zone alone.

One of the surviving paratroop companies advanced towards what they regarded as a 'tent encampment' on the coast north-east of Galatas. It was, in fact, a military hospital containing hundreds of patients, with New Zealand's 6th Field Ambulance near by. However, despite extensive marking with red crosses, the area had been heavily bombed in the morning's air raids (although the Red Cross was respected by the Germans throughout the rest of the battle). German intelligence seems to have identified only part of the site as a medical facility, and apparently regarded the many tents as a military camp because men wearing helmets and carrying arms had been seen passing through it.

The paratroop company occupied the area and took the orderlies and patients prisoner. Unfortunately, the commander of 6th Field Ambulance, Lieutenant Colonel Plimmer, was killed at the moment of surrender. An eyewitness has suggested that as Plimmer climbed out of a trench his hand inadvertently dropped towards his holster and a nervous paratrooper then shot him.[18] Soon after the colonel's burial, the German commander decided to escort the 500 orderlies and mobile patients toward Galatas, where he felt he would find other airborne units. But moving such a large column of sick, injured and frightened men proved a

Below left: Soldiers from the 18th Battalion with a dead paratrooper.
[ATL: DA-14595]

Below right: A Red Cross flag at the military hospital north of Galatas.
[ATL: DA-11712]

disaster, as it was quickly ambushed by soldiers from the 19th Battalion. The German guards were killed, along with some of those they had taken prisoner, although most of the latter were freed, shaken but unharmed.

South of Galatas two paratroop battalions (over 1,000 men) had landed in the lightly defended Prison Valley and were soon in action against the Greek regiments stationed near by. One of the regiments, poorly armed and short of ammunition, was pushed back into the New Zealand lines, but the 8th Greek Regiment, below Lake Aghya, held their ground, and were quickly joined by local Cretans, 'women and children among them and armed mainly with shotguns'.[19] Re-equipped with modern weapons taken from dead Germans and parachute containers, these Greek soldiers and Cretan irregulars blocked the enemy advance for several days. Beevor considers that their resistance against a German move through the foothills eventually saved Freyberg's force from 'almost certain encirclement and a humiliating surrender'.[20]

Other Cretans also rushed to join the battle, as Theoharis Mylonakis recalled:

> My 60 year old father dug up a long Manliher gun which he had not handed in during the Metaxas arms requisition. He too wanted to go and fight. It was only when I told him that I too had to enlist, even without a weapon, that he gave it to me. Clutching both my doctor's kit and the gun in one hand, I put 20–25 bullets in my jacket pocket. I was not even sure they were unused.[21]

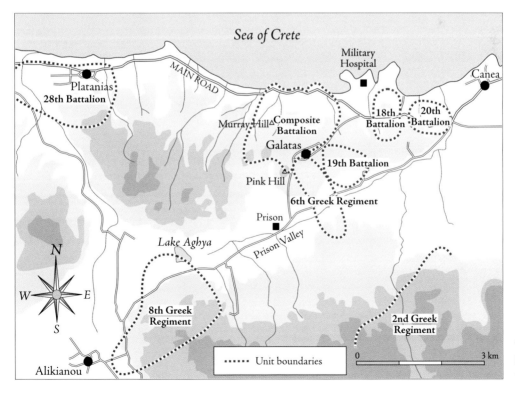

Map: Allied positions in the Galatas sector.

Some of the Cretans and Greek soldiers were put under the command of a British officer, Michael Forrester, who gave them some rudimentary training when they were in Galatas. They would serve bravely in the upcoming battle for the small hills around the village.

By mid-morning the paratroopers were advancing from the valley up through the olive trees covering the nearby slopes. At a point called 'Pink Hill' (because of the colour of its earth), they encountered Kiwis from the Divisional Petrol Company now fighting as infantry. After a bloody battle the enemy took the hill (which they later abandoned, possibly fearing a strong counter-attack), but the rest of the Allied line was stabilised and a breakthrough averted.

Colonel Kippenberger, who was in charge of this sector, believed that a robust assault into the Prison Valley would force the Germans back and possibly crush them. He pressed Brigadier Puttick, now in command of the New Zealand Division, to release some of the reserve battalions, arguing that 'a vigorous counter-attack would clear the prison'.[22] Over the afternoon, Brigadier Inglis and other officers supported his case, but Puttick continued to hesitate. Paratroopers had landed everywhere, in various strengths, and no doubt Puttick was anxious that more might suddenly arrive, or that a landing could come from the sea. He also believed he might have to reinforce the Maleme sector, rather than Galatas, where he felt that 'all that was required was to hold fast'.[23] Critically, as it transpired, he waited and thus the chance to defeat a large part of the invading force faded. Kippenberger would later tersely criticise Puttick's behaviour:

> He was baffled. When asked to counterattack he replied with platitudes, with last-war maxims, and with generalities about war which have no application to the case in point. And he did next to nothing.[24]

Right: A street in Canea is used as a holding area for German prisoners.

[ATL: DA-01153]

Above left: Peter McIntyre painting a mural in the New Zealand Forces Club in Cairo. [ATL: DA-00952]
Above right: Peter McIntyre, 'Parachutists landing on Galatas'. [Archives New Zealand, AAAC 898 NCWA 16]

A WAR ARTIST IN ACTION

The New Zealand official war artist, Peter McIntyre, arrived in Suda Bay a few days before the battle commenced, having personally asked Freyberg for permission to join the forces in Crete. After doing some sketches of the Greek king, McIntyre was at the 4th Brigade headquarters on the day of the invasion. He watched the transport planes approaching and the paratroopers dropping, 'in cluster after cluster, like puffs opening into a cloud of monster thistledown'.

At one point McIntyre was sitting behind a stone wall, observing the parachutes coming down around Galatas. He was attempting a watercolour of the dramatic scene, when a Kiwi soldier came up to him:

He was about to pass on when he saw that I was painting a watercolour. He did a double-take and stared for a while. I looked him fair in the eye but he just shook his head, said, 'She's right, Dig. P'raps I'm nuts.' and went on his way.

After suffering under the constant bombing and strafing alongside the other soldiers, McIntyre would write: 'I saw men with glazed eyes as I never saw again in all the rest of the war.' Eventually, carrying a rifle, ammunition, tins of bully beef and, most importantly, his sketches, he joined the column retreating from Suda Bay over the mountains to Sfakia. With no official photographers and cameramen alongside the New Zealand forces on Crete, he knew he had to get his work to Cairo.

Arriving on the south coast footsore and exhausted, McIntyre waited in a cave, knowing that war artists were not high on the list to be taken off. Fortunately, he found a spare place on a barge that took him out to a Royal Navy destroyer and then on to Egypt.

Back at Maadi camp, McIntyre's sketches were immediately published in a magazine and his paintings were exhibited in Cairo. His work was soon well known in the Middle East and in New Zealand; as he later wrote, 'to become known as a war artist is one of those breaks that can make an artist for life'.[25]

PETER McINTYRE

Eventually, as the evening approached, two counter-attacks were finally put in. First, Inglis, off his own bat, sent an infantry company in an unsuccessful attempt to retake a position lost by a gun battery. Then Puttick, after receiving information (later shown to be unfounded) that the Germans were building an airstrip near the prison, at last decided to act. At dusk two companies from the 19th Battalion and three light tanks under the command of Roy Farran were sent into the valley. Three hours later, having destroyed some German pockets, they came to a halt in the dark. Meanwhile Kippenberger, who learnt about the plan only when the tanks were rolling through Galatas, had decided that the force was too weak and the attack had started too late to reach the prison. He ordered an end to the advance and the companies and tanks withdrew. The unsettled battlefield finally fell quiet.

Below: The remains of a paratrooper who landed at the military hospital and was killed in a burning tent. The Allied soldier is holding a German pistol.

[ATL: DA-01108]

Thus a stalemate of sorts had been reached in the Galatas sector by the end of the first day of battle, but at Maleme things were falling apart for the Allies. As the hours wore on Lieutenant Colonel Andrew had become increasingly pessimistic about the prospects of his forward companies, while at distant Platanias, Brigadier Hargest remained out of touch with the worrying realities on the ground at Maleme.

When the air raid preceding the invasion occurred, Hargest had been in Platanias village. He had just written in his diary, 'No breakfast, feeling a little tired so will take things easier today', when the raid began.[26] He was forced 'to dash and crawl through a storm of machine gun fire from enemy aeroplanes in order to reach his Battle HQ' on the hill above the village.[27] From there he could see the heavy bombing around the airfield and the arrival of the airborne assault force. Unfortunately, the telephone line to the 22nd Battalion was soon cut and from then on communications with Andrew depended on radio contact, which became intermittent as batteries ran down. Andrew was able to inform Hargest about the scale of the German attack, however, as well as his own problems in maintaining communications with his companies.

Meanwhile the commanders of the 23rd and 21st battalions, Leckie and Allen, both told Hargest that they had overcome the paratroopers who had landed around their positions and that their areas east of Maleme were under control. At 2.25 p.m. an optimistic Hargest sent a signal

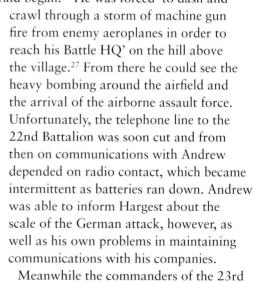

to Leckie, saying: 'Will NOT call on you for counter-attacking unless position very serious. So far everything is in hand and reports from other units satisfactory.'[28]

Yet for Andrew matters were becoming increasingly unsatisfactory, and by 4 p.m. he had sent anxious messages to Hargest, informing him that the Germans were penetrating his lines and that reinforcements were badly needed. An hour later he specifically asked the brigadier to set in motion the pre-arranged plan for the 23rd Battalion to counter-attack towards the airfield. Hargest made the surprising reply that the 23rd could not carry out such a move because it was busy fighting the paratroops.

Nothing could have been further from the truth. Since eliminating the Germans who had landed in and around its area, the soldiers of the 23rd had had a relatively quiet day. Their officers waited for a request from Andrew or an order from Hargest to move towards Maleme. Although the telephone line between the battalions was cut, there were other attempts at communication. Signallers at the 22nd Battalion sent up flares requesting assistance but they were not seen, probably because of the dust and smoke. Leckie did send a platoon to try to make contact with the 22nd, but the latter's soldiers, thinking the approaching men were Germans, kept them at bay with rifle and mortar fire. Historian Tony Simpson, on the basis of an account told 40 years later, wrote that Andrew himself made his way to the 23rd Battalion to request a counter-attack but was rejected. However, with no other supporting statements, either at the time or later, and no documentary record, it is almost certain this event did not occur.[29] For now, Andrew remained on his hill.

Why Hargest thought the 23rd Battalion was back in action remains a mystery, but his negative response to Andrew's request for the planned counter-attack meant that the colonel had to fall back on his own meagre resources. He ordered an assault by the two tanks (a type known as 'Matildas') hidden on the slopes of Point 107, supported by an infantry platoon, but for an unknown reason, instead of attacking the Germans around the airfield, the tanks headed into the Tavronitis riverbed. Haddon Donald, the platoon commander, later recalled the chaos that ensued:

> We followed the Matildas down the road, watched one of them get to the bridge itself. We were being shot at all the time, I got a bullet through my leg and several of my platoon boys were wounded, one or two killed. We saw the first tank become immobilised under the bridge and the men get out and surrender to the Germans. The second tank came back along the road towards us . . . his turret was jammed with a splinter of steel which I saw and so he was pulling back . . . by that time we had only eight left of our 26 men who hadn't been wounded or killed. We put some of the wounded on to the tank itself and sheltered behind it and pulled back to our company's headquarters.[30]

The terror that the tanks should have struck in the lightly armed airborne troops had been wasted. The commander of C Company (Captain Johnson) then sent a runner to Andrew to tell him that this limited counter-attack had failed and that the other C Company platoons were crumbling under the constant German pressure.

Above: Hargest (right) at Platanias.

[ATL: DA-12180]

He said he could probably hold on till nightfall, but would then need immediate reinforcement.

Andrew, out of touch with half of his companies, must have felt he had no reinforcements to offer. Around 6 p.m. he contacted Hargest, told him the tank attack had not been successful and that, if there was to be no support from the 23rd Battalion, he would have to pull back from Point 107. Hargest made the fateful reply, which would ultimately ensure the loss of Crete, 'well, if you must, you must'.[31] Five minutes later he was back on the radio with the promise that two infantry companies would be sent to support the 22nd Battalion, but he did not order Andrew to stay in position until they arrived.

Andrew later said that he expected the companies, one from the 28th Maori Battalion and the other from the 23rd, to arrive almost immediately. There seems to have been no urgency in their orders, however, and they did not set off until 7.30 p.m. When the company from the 23rd finally found Andrew two hours later he had already made a partial withdrawal from Point 107 to a nearby ridge. The Maori company, which had to cover a much longer distance over unfamiliar ground, was soon lost in the dark; they took to talking and singing in te reo so they would not be fired on by other Kiwi units.

By late evening an increasingly tired and stressed Andrew believed (wrongly, as it turned out) that only two companies from his battalion were still intact. Runners had been sent to find the others but, descending into the fearsome dark, had located no one. Even when the men from the 23rd finally arrived, Andrew must have decided that an additional company was not enough to restore the situation. Having concluded that once daylight came his new position would be indefensible against ground and air attack, he withdrew his force to the east where they linked up with the 21st and 23rd battalions.

Right: The bridge over the Tavronitis River.

[David Filer]

But Andrew's companies around the airfield and above the river, although depleted, had not been wiped out. They were awaiting orders from battalion headquarters, but none arrived. In the early hours of 21 May, C and D companies separately sent men to the top of Point 107, only to find the positions abandoned. C Company then pulled out, but the sceptical commander of D Company (Captain Campbell) sent his runner up the hill again. When he returned to confirm that battalion headquarters had gone, D Company carefully withdrew, as the unit history relates:

> Every man removed his boots and hung them round his neck. Critically wounded men were made as comfortable as possible and left with food and water. The southern wire . . . was cut and, in single file, the wounded interspersed here and there, they set off . . . They went past the snoring Germans to the right, through the vineyards separating C Company from A Company, up to A Company's deserted headquarters, on to the road, up the hill past a grounded and ghostly glider until, after dawn, they reached a wood near 21 Battalion's positions. As they fell dead-tired under the trees, German planes began the morning hate.[32]

Andrew's reaction to finding that his 'lost' companies had survived is not known, although he was no doubt both relieved and disconcerted. But it did not alter his belief that he had made the right decision to withdraw, as he later wrote in the battalion's war diary:

> Even if the position could have been restored by a counter-attack it could not have been held even by a fresh battalion. Looking back now and knowing more of the facts I am convinced that the withdrawal at the time was the only possible action to take.[33]

Before C and D companies had arrived, the commanders of the 21st and 23rd battalions (Allen and Leckie) and the local artillery commander (Major Philp) had met with Andrew. Philp noted that 'all looked to Colonel Andrew', despite his haggard and exhausted appearance.[34] He was, after all, an experienced Regular soldier, a Victoria Cross winner, and his battalion had taken the brunt of the action that day. Furthermore, there had been no guidance or orders from Hargest, who had not moved closer to the action, even though the debilitating air attacks had ceased once night fell.

None of the assembled commanders expressed any enthusiasm for launching an immediate counter-attack. Instead they decided to hold their present positions while the battered 22nd Battalion reorganised.

As everyone desperately tried to grab a few hours of sleep, the only sounds from Maleme were the frogs which 'croaked incessantly among the sedges by the river, and there was a mournful braying from a group of donkeys still tethered among the trees beyond the bridge'.[35]

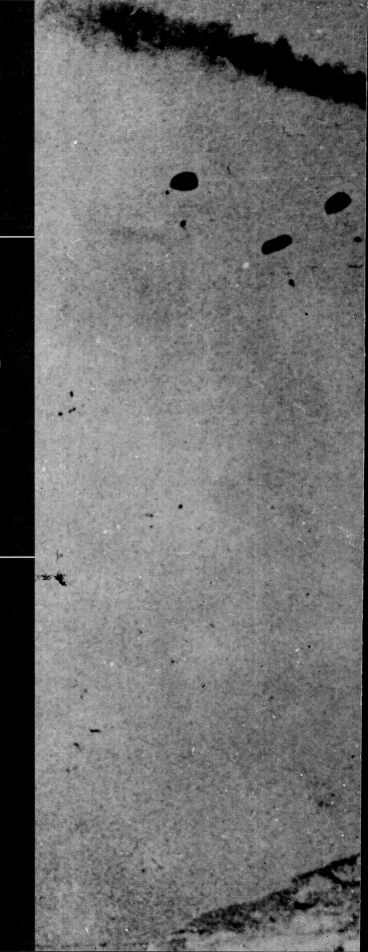

1941

20 MAY

8 A.M.

Kastelli Kisamou: German
paratroopers land

Kastelli Kisamou: Germans defeated

NOON

4 P.M. Retimo: German paratroopers land

Heraklion: German paratroopers land

Retimo: Germans capture Hill 'A'

8 P.M.

20 MAY

MIDNIGHT Canea: Freyberg cables Wavell

21 MAY

4 A.M.

8 A.M.

Retimo: Germans driven off Hill 'A'

5

DAY ONE: RETIMO, HERAKLION AND KASTELLI KISAMOU

The second wave of the airborne invasion of Crete was planned to arrive at Retimo and Heraklion around 2 p.m. on 20 May, but the aircraft were delayed because of slow refuelling and the clouds of dust created by landings and departures on the Greek airfields. In addition, some of the Junker 52s which had carried the first wave had been damaged by ground fire and needed repairs before they could take off again.

Eventually, following a brief air raid, the Luftwaffe's transport planes appeared over Retimo at 4.15 p.m. and began dropping 1,500 paratroopers. Their main target was the airfield, next to the coast road eight kilometres out of town. It was overlooked by low hills occupied by two tough and experienced Australian battalions (under the command of Lieutenant Colonel Campbell and Major Sandover), which were supported by some poorly armed Greek units. The town itself was defended by the Cretan police and, once the battle began, local civilians.

Campbell had made sure the Australian positions were well camouflaged and, as at Maleme and Galatas, many of the paratroopers were dropped directly over them and were killed or captured immediately. Unlike Maleme, however, the anti-aircraft defence around Retimo airfield was also effective and seven Junkers were soon shot down. Other planes veered across the sea, releasing their troops into the waves where they drowned.

Some Germans were lucky to be dropped in a wrong but relatively safe location around an olive oil factory two kilometres east of the airfield. They quickly moved towards the main hill (known as 'Hill A'), gathering up other paratroopers in their path. With typical determination they stormed up the slopes, pushing the Australian defenders back from the crest.

Campbell knew that Hill A was the key position to holding the airfield and, with a decisiveness in stark contrast to Andrew and Hargest at Maleme, he ordered an immediate counter-attack. But his 'Matilda' tanks also failed and, although

Previous page: A troop transport on fire over Heraklion. [ATL: DA-02061]

Below left: Paratroopers before the invasion of Crete. [E. Neville]

Below right: Australian soldiers who fought on Crete. [Australian War Memorial: 007742/31]

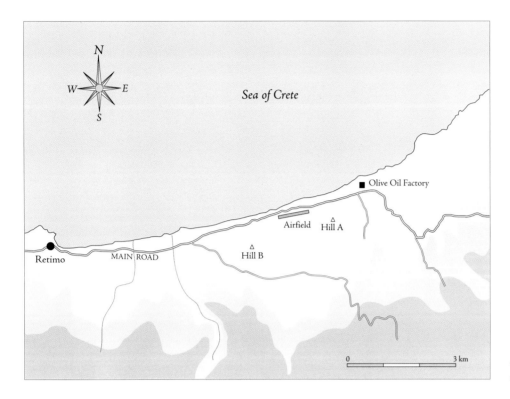

Map: Key locations in the battle at Retimo.

the defence line was stabilised, the Germans remained on the hill. In response to a radio signal to Freyberg asking for reinforcements, Campbell received only this brief reply: 'Regret unable to send help. Good luck.'[1]

The colonel was not disheartened, however, and planned another counter-attack for first light on the following day. When that failed he threw in all his reserves, including the Greek regiments. The Germans were rattled when their own aircraft bombed them by mistake and soon after the Australians swept them off the hill.

The paratroop commander then pulled his men back to the olive oil factory, which he turned into a strongly fortified position. Another group of Germans dug in around a church and other buildings outside Retimo. The Cretans attacked the entrenchments, including a suicidal charge across open ground, but could not overcome the defenders.

For most of the rest of the battle the Germans remained trapped in these positions, with ammunition, food and water in short supply. One paratrooper recalled the terrible conditions:

> We had left our rations with our tunics somewhere or other because of the heat. Water was to be had only in the adjoining factory . . . we found wine in the cellar of a hut. I had it rationed out in sips, otherwise men would have got drunk instantly through exhaustion and the awful thirst. To assuage hunger we cut ears of corn and chewed the grains. An ownerless goat which strayed to us was slaughtered on the spot.[2]

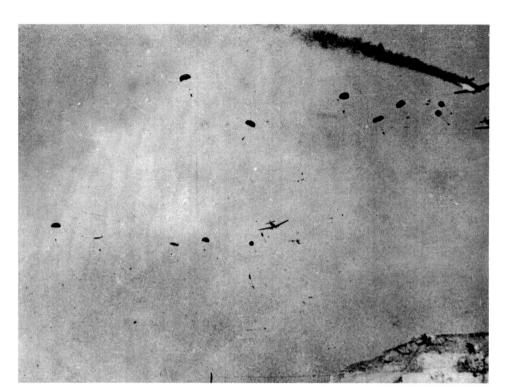

Right: Paratroopers dropping near Heraklion. One of the transport planes has been hit by anti-aircraft fire. [ATL: DA-02061]

The Australians, Greeks and Cretans, with dynamic leadership, had prevented the Germans from taking either the airfield or port at Retimo. They had captured hundreds of paratroopers, and many more were casualties. An Australian soldier later reflected on the tragedy of war:

> War is really horrible but once in close combat it is kill or be killed. On 21st and 22nd May, when we were burying the dead, I looked at a little wallet of the first man I had shot, a parachute Hauptmann [Captain], and in it was a photo of his wife and five-year-old daughter. I thought things could have been in reverse, as I also had a photo of my wife and daughter in my wallet.[3]

Further east, at Heraklion, in an odd oversight the Allied commander, Brigadier Chappel, was not informed by Creforce headquarters that the battle for the island had actually begun until around 2.30 p.m. So when the paratroopers started to land around the city and its airport three hours later, a number of officers were still away from their units. But all defenders were soon firing at the men dangling in the sky above them and, as in the other sectors, easily killed many invaders in the air or immediately their feet touched the ground. With black humour, some British officers compared the slaughter to a grouse shoot back home.[4]

General Student had made the same mistake at Heraklion as he had for the entire invasion, spreading his forces too thinly across the battle zone. Around 2,000 paratroopers were dropped along a 20-kilometre stretch of coast running from the east to the west of the city. Twice that number of British troops awaited them, augmented by an Australian battalion, Greek regiments and Cretan police. They were supported by camouflaged anti-aircraft guns (which shot down fifteen planes), artillery and tanks.

Two groups of Germans were dropped well away from Heraklion, one to capture a wireless station and the other to block the coast road to the west, while the main force targeted the airfield and the port. The battalion that landed around the airfield was soon largely destroyed, with Chappel making effective use of his tanks in an immediate counter-attack. The lightly armed paratroopers were easy prey; one British officer reported that they were shot 'by the revolvers of his tank commanders, and many others were killed by running over them'.[5]

When another battalion dropped just outside the city, its citizens rallied to its defence, as Christos Bantouvas recalled:

> We ran to the warehouse . . . where the guns were stored, broke down the door, took the weapons and stood guard outside, waiting for the aircraft. Upon their arrival we opened fire. The Germans who dropped down onto this area were too numerous to mention and they fired continuously at us . . . We of course killed as many as possible.[6]

However, despite determined resistance from Cretans and Greek soldiers on the old Venetian walls and in the narrow streets, the paratroopers fought their way into the city and moved towards the port. Eventually, British reinforcements arrived to halt the Germans' advance and, with ammunition low, they pulled out of the city. They and their compatriots east of the airfield remained holed up for the rest of the battle, too spent to advance but not weak enough to have to surrender. They were frustrated at watching the Luftwaffe drop essential supplies over Allied positions. As the Kiwis and Aussies in the other sectors had also learnt, if captured swastika flags were laid on the ground, food, medicine, ammunition and weapons would soon fall from the sky, courtesy of the Third Reich. The hungry and thirsty paratroopers could only grit their teeth and hope for deliverance.

At Heraklion, Chappel had shown the same determination and drive as Campbell at Retimo, and well-planned defences and a rapid counter-attack had once again prevented the Germans from taking an important airfield and a useful port.

There was one further paratroop landing on 20 May, when a small detachment of around 70 men was dropped near the far western port of Kastelli Kisamou. It was their misfortune to be immediately attacked by local Cretans, along with the Greek regiment that Freyberg and Puttick had earlier considered moving to Maleme (see page 50). The Greeks (who were being trained by New Zealand instructors under Major Bedding) showed reckless courage, and suffered over 100 casualties before the German force was annihilated.

When the handful of German survivors were rounded up, the Cretans wanted to immediately execute them, but Bedding made sure they were protected and imprisoned. (Ironically, a few days later, after a bombing raid, some of the paratroopers escaped and then held Bedding prisoner until German reinforcements eventually arrived and took the town.)

The first day of the battle of Crete had been a frustrating one for Major General Freyberg. He was used to being near the front line where he could use his long experience to get an instinctive 'feel' for how the fight was going. Instead he had been stuck at Creforce headquarters on the hill above Canea, relying on third and fourth-hand reports of the far-flung operations.

Understandably, it took some time to sort through and make sense of the often confused and contradictory information arriving from the various sectors. By the evening, however, a clearer picture was emerging, greatly assisted by the capture of a German document which contained a summary of Student's entire plan. Geoffrey Cox, who could read German, had found it in a mass of enemy material and, realising its significance, had taken it to Freyberg:

> The General sat behind a bare wooden trestle table in his dugout. On the table lay a hand grenade ready for use against any enemy intruder. With John White holding a torch for me to read by, I made a rough translation of the order. It not only gave in detail the plans for the 3rd Parachute Regiment, but also a summary of the invasion plan for the whole island, including the attack on Retimo and Heraklion.[7]

As well as proving to Freyberg that the Germans had failed to achieve their objectives, it also showed how badly they had underestimated the size of the Allied force defending Crete. But Freyberg was a realist and knew that the battle had only just begun, and towards midnight, in a level-headed cable to General Wavell in Egypt, he stated his views on Day One:

> Today has been a hard one. We have been hard pressed. I believe that so far we hold the aerodromes at Maleme, Heraklion and Retimo and the two harbours. The margin by which we hold them is a bare one and it would be wrong of me to paint an optimistic picture. The fighting has been heavy and large numbers of Germans have been killed. Communications are most difficult. The scale of air attack upon us has been severe. Everybody here realises the vital issue and we will fight it out.[8]

Unfortunately, what Freyberg did not know was that at Maleme airfield Lieutenant Colonel Andrew appeared to have lost sight of the 'vital issue' and was no longer fighting it out.

CRETE NEWS

One of the most unusual newspapers ever produced was published four times on Crete before and during the battle. It was called *Crete News* and was established at General Freyberg's instigation in 'an attempt to boost morale and to stem rumour-mongering'.[9] Soon after arriving on the island he had told Second Lieutenant Geoffrey Cox, a New Zealander who in civilian life had been a famous foreign correspondent for leading British dailies, to quickly create a newspaper for the troops.

Cox faced and overcame some daunting problems. He convinced the owner of the Canea evening paper to also print the *Crete News*, a supply of newsprint was provided by Prince Peter of Greece and, with the troops unable to read Greek lettering, two cases of French type were luckily found on a boat that had just arrived from Athens. Cox also procured the services of some Kiwi journalists and printers enlisted in the division, along with a Greek journalist and compositor. Rounding out the staff were an English schoolteacher and the local paper's compositors, a Cretan man and his two daughters.

Photographic blocks for Greek papers showing British soldiers, ships and planes provided the illustrations and a woodcarver cut another block for the paper's title, while international news was obtained by listening to the BBC.

The first edition was nearly a flop when the Cretan printer refused to take orders from the Athenian journalist, but Cox was able to convince the printer that a New Zealander was actually in charge. Despite the disruption of an air raid, production was completed in the early hours of 16 May and the paper was immediately distributed to the troops around the island.

The next edition came out just before the invasion and the third two days after the battle had begun. Cox included his own summary of the production problems:

Crete News will continue publishing throughout the Blitz so long as the printing press remains undamaged. We cannot guarantee as prompt delivery as in earlier times. We print no news from the outside world because all radios were being used yesterday for the battle. Besides for the present in the outside world the Battle for Crete is the news.[10]

The last edition was typeset and printed on 24 May in the midst of a huge air raid on Canea. The newsprint was rescued from a burning shed, the compositors had to work in a cave full of people taking refuge from the attack and, just after the edition was printed, the newspaper building was hit by a bomb. Six hundred copies were still produced, but unfortunately they were dumped during the withdrawal and only a few survived.

Crete News remains a unique publication. As Cox later wrote: 'There can be few instances in World War II when troops learnt of the progress of a battle in which they were engaged from a newspaper which was delivered to them in action.'[11]

Above: The front page of the fourth, and last, edition of Crete News.

[ATL: DA-06854]

1941
20 MAY
MIDNIGHT
21 MAY

Germans capture Point 107

8 A.M.   German paratroop reserves land west
of Maleme

NOON

Counter-attack conference

5 P.M.   Mountain troops land at Maleme

11 P.M.   Royal Navy intercepts first German flotilla
MIDNIGHT
22 MAY

Luftwaffe bombing of Royal Navy
ships begins
Royal Navy intercepts second
German flotilla

NOON

6

DESPERATE
MEASURES

If Freyberg had endured a difficult first day of battle, it paled in comparison to the problems faced by Student and the other German generals at their headquarters in Athens. Student's staff was in radio contact with the airborne forces near Maleme, below Galatas and outside Heraklion, but not with Retimo. He knew that many of his commanders had been killed or wounded and, therefore, that casualties among all their units had to be heavy. Worst of all, none of the key targets, the airfields or ports, had been taken.

By late evening some of the officers at the headquarters had begun to express doubts about continuing with the operation and Student's intelligence chief asked him if he should start considering how to break off the engagement. But the general, no doubt aware that his career was on the line, was made of sterner stuff.

Knowing that a substantial force had landed west of Maleme and had gained a bridgehead over the Tavronitis River, he decided to concentrate all his remaining units in that sector. As Stewart has written:

> . . . it is true that [Student] had kept his nerve better than the whisperers who surrounded him, and that he came at last to his 'decisive resolution', choosing the one course that might still retrieve the earlier mistakes and save the battle, 'I decided to use the mass of my parachute reserve still at my disposal for the final capture of Maleme aerodrome'.[1]

Previous page: German mountain troops board an aircraft before flying to Crete. [Filer collection]

Below: German officers at Student's headquarters in Athens. [Australian War Memorial: 072856]

Before he went to bed, Student resolved to obtain some clear information on what was happening around the airfield. He ordered a 'bold, go-getting character on my staff', Captain Kleye, to fly to Crete in the early morning and land at Maleme, 'to get a personal feeling of how things were going'.[2]

Meanwhile, as Andrew and his companies were abandoning the defences at the airfield, an aggressive German medical officer made a brave but seemingly foolhardy decision to storm Point 107. He gathered up some determined paratroopers, survived a friendly firefight and charged up the hill. He and his men must have been astonished to find the enemy gone and the key position in their hands.

Not long after, Kleye, unaware that Point 107 had fallen, briefly touched down and took off at the airfield. He was able to report back to Student that although he was shot at from a distance, the western end of the airstrip was 'dead ground', protected from direct fire. Student immediately ordered some of his paratroop reserve, 350 men, to be dropped in the German-held area near the Tavronitis. Another six planes were despatched to land on a nearby beach with ammunition and supplies, although taking off again among the rocks and sand would prove difficult.

In mid-afternoon the reinforced airborne troops moved forward. They passed the airfield and took Maleme village, but their advance was brought to a halt near the next hamlet by machine gun and rifle fire from the 23rd Battalion. At the same time Student dropped the last of his paratroopers four kilometres to the east, along the coast road towards Platanias. In another painful example of poor German intelligence and reconnaissance, the companies fell on top of the Maori Battalion and a Kiwi engineer detachment, who had killed some of their comrades the day before. Again, many of the new invaders were shot in the air and on the ground, while some who dropped into the sea drowned.

As the battle raged, Student decided to risk sending a battalion of soldiers from the 5th Mountain Division to land on Maleme airfield. New Zealand gunners were shelling the runway and the pilots of the Junker 52s found they were descending into a scene of chaos, with planes being hit, crash-landing or smashing into each other. Some aircraft had no choice but to try to land on the vine terraces or the road alongside the airfield. One soldier described his terrifying arrival:

> The JU just manages to jump over a vine, touches ground, rears up and digs with one wing into the ground. Grinding under the huge pressure it breaks asunder in the middle and rips the fuselage half a turn to the left. Men, packs, life jackets, ammunition are thrown forward, torn and squeezed tightly . . . then the JU comes to a halt half standing on its head. But we still grip our rifles. None have been hurt. 'Out!' someone calls.[3]

Some of soldiers were immediately sent into action while others prepared to defend the airfield from a counter-attack. The German commanders were willing to lose planes in order to get their men on the ground and soon 20 aircraft were destroyed

Left: Crashed planes at Maleme airfield with Point 107 to the rear.
[ATL: DA-11971]

and the runway was cluttered with wrecks. The officers in charge of the airfield used a captured Bren-gun carrier to clear the debris, and prisoners of war were forced to assist. Three men who refused were summarily executed.

A New Zealand soldier, watching from a distance, described the 'inferno' at Maleme:

> The aerodrome was covered with crashed and burning planes. It was obscured at intervals by dust and smoke. It was being shelled quite heavily by our guns and we could see them getting direct hits on planes as they landed . . . In spite of all this the big German planes were coming down steadily and landing in the smoke and explosions.[4]

Nearly 800 soldiers were brought in through the airfield before nightfall on 21 May. Along with the surviving airborne forces who had arrived that day and the previous one, there were now around 2,000 German fighting men in the Maleme sector.

When Brigadier Hargest had gone to bed at his Platanias headquarters on the night of 20 May he had been in a confident mood. Although he had given Lieutenant Colonel Andrew permission to abandon Point 107, he must have thought that the two companies he was sending to support Andrew would stabilise the line, because at 9.45 p.m., in a message to the New Zealand Division, he stated that the situation in his sector was 'quite satisfactory'.[5] Having made no attempt to go up to Maleme, the brigadier had no understanding of the disaster unfolding in his key defence zone.

Hargest received a real shock, therefore, when Major Leggat, the second-in-command of the 22nd Battalion, arrived at his headquarters in the early hours of 21 May. Leggat reported 'that we were officially off Maleme', and the brigadier,

Right: The view from a New Zealand position as fires burn at Maleme airfield. [ATL: DA-10999]

Left: 5th Brigade officers at Platanias, including Hargest (front centre) and (behind him) Andrew.
[ATL: DA-07513]

just awakened and still in pyjamas, 'was absolutely surprised and unprepared'.[6] However, he did not set off for the front line, even after Andrew came to see him at 5 a.m. The earlier decision of the battalion commanders to hold their positions and fit the men from the 22nd Battalion inside them was simply confirmed. There was no discussion of an immediate counter-attack.

An hour earlier Hargest had informed divisional headquarters about the withdrawal from Point 107 and the airfield, which was then passed on to Creforce. Freyberg knew immediately that a counter-attack was required to retake the Maleme positions but, because of German air power, it would have to occur at night. In the afternoon he held a conference with the New Zealand brigadiers Puttick and Inglis and the Australian commander Vasey, although Hargest did not attend. Discussion centred around which units were available for the counter-attack, as many troops were already in action holding the lines at Galatas and east of Maleme, while others were protecting the coast against a possible sea landing. Although a number of units potentially could take part, the conference concluded that a two-battalion attack, using the Maori Battalion near Platanias and the 20th Battalion west of Canea, should be enough. The Australian 2/7th Battalion at Georgeoupolis was considered, but Vasey wanted to keep his units together, and the commanders decided that it would instead take over coastal defences held by the 20th Battalion.

One of the great debates among Crete veterans and historians has concerned the planned German invasion from the sea and whether this threat distracted Freyberg and his subordinates from putting in an effective and timely counter-attack at Maleme. British historians like Ian Stewart and Antony Beevor consider that Freyberg was overly focused on the threat from the sea before and during the battle and that this was a primary reason for the Allied defeat on Crete. In this regard, Stewart noted that Freyberg wrote a letter to Churchill after the war was over, stating that 'we, for our part, were mostly preoccupied by sea-landings, not by the threat of air-landings'.[7] However, this remark by Freyberg related mainly to his early concerns about support from the navy[8] (see below); it does not match up with his statements and the orders given to his forces in the days before the battle.

Freyberg's initial anxiety after taking command on Crete was that the Royal Navy did not have the resources to intercept an invasion fleet, but he soon accepted that the navy would do its best, despite the threat to its warships from Luftwaffe bombers. His main concern then centred on how to deal with a sea landing if it occurred at the same time as the invasion from the air. As he told Wavell in mid-May:

> If they come as an airborne attack against our aerodromes, I feel sure we should be able to stop him if he attacks after the 16th. If however he makes a combined operation of it with a beach landing with tanks, then we shall not be in a strong position.[9]

A number of other documents indicate that Freyberg regarded the air invasion as the main threat, with the sea landing of lesser significance. In particular, the Creforce summary of the German plan of attack, issued to senior commanders on 12 May, stated that sea landings 'will be of secondary importance to those from the air'.[10] Most of the Ultra secret intelligence that Freyberg received before 20 May in fact related to the airborne assault and its support by the Luftwaffe. But he also had been informed that the Germans were planning to bring a substantial force to Crete by sea, including troops, supplies, anti-aircraft guns and tanks, with the likely date for the landing being the second day of the battle.[11]

Right: Kiwis on a beach in the Gulf of Canea before the invasion.

[ATL: DA-10650]

Accordingly, while Freyberg placed his primary emphasis on defending the key targets — the airfields and ports — all the units near the coast had to be ready to repel both air and seaborne invasions. It has been suggested since the war, however, that around Canea, because of the shallow water and rocky coast, a seaborne landing would have been almost impossible. Beevor has written that 'only the beach from Maleme to Platanias could have been considered possible for a landing in any strength and then only if the Germans had assault ships and landing craft, which they did not'.[12]

In fact, it appears that the Germans were planning an old-fashioned attack from the sea, with their first waves of troops either using small boats to row to the beach from ships standing off the coast (a method that Freyberg would have remembered from Gallipoli in 1915) or clambering off vessels that could reach shallow water. Any beach west of Canea would be open to either style of landing, provided it was undefended. Freyberg would have been aware, however, that the Germans would not be able to bring in heavy equipment through a beach landing and instead would have to seize a port like Canea.

This may explain why he appeared to take little notice of information appended to the German operational order translated by Geoffrey Cox on the night of 20 May (see page 80), which stated that a sea landing would occur on the undefended beaches west of Maleme. He was much more excited by some secret intelligence that arrived at Creforce on 21 May, apparently as the conference to discuss the counter-attack to retake Maleme airfield was winding up. This information stated that it had been:

> . . . reliably reported that among operations planned for Twenty-first May is air landing two mountain battalions and attack Canea. Landing from echelon of small ships depending on situation at sea.[13]

Beevor has argued that Freyberg confused the two sentences, thereby misunderstanding the intelligence. Instead of interpreting the attack on Canea as a move by troops already on the ground (or as an air raid), he assumed that there would be a seaborne assault to take the port. Brigadier Inglis wrote that Freyberg warned the conference of an imminent seaborne landing west of Canea and the general later sent out a signal stating: 'Reliable information. Early seaborne attack in area Canea likely.'[14] In fact, there was no such plan.

Beevor considers that Freyberg's misinterpretation was 'the main element in the disastrous train of events which befell the counter-attack on Maleme planned for the same night'.[15] However, he exaggerates its effect on the size of the force chosen for the operation, as this decision had been made before the Ultra information arrived. The real impact was on the replacement of the 20th Battalion in its coastal defences by the Australian 2/7th Battalion, as the delays which occurred while this was taking place caused a crucial change in the start time for the entire counter-attack, a factor which would have significant repercussions.

As the conference at Creforce headquarters broke up, the Australian commander of the 2/7th Battalion pointed out to Brigadier Inglis the problems with the plan, namely, the difficulties of bringing forward, by night, 'a battalion that lacked its own transport, was eighteen miles away, was not connected to headquarters by telephone, in time for it to relieve another battalion that was to make an attack the same night'. Inglis had tersely replied that 'a well-trained battalion could carry out such a relief in an hour'.[16] But events would prove the Aussie right.

While Freyberg and his commanders were making their decisions, the invasion force was at sea, chugging slowly across the Aegean towards Crete. It was less imposing than anyone could have imagined and is another example of the arrogance and foolhardiness of the Axis plans. Hitler, however, had insisted on a sea landing to support the airborne troops.

In mid-May the Germans had assembled around 60 requisitioned vessels in Piraeus harbour to carry two battalions of soldiers from the 5th Mountain Division, some paratroopers, anti-aircraft guns, ammunition and other supplies to Crete. The vessels were mainly the ubiquitous Greek fishing and trading schooner (the caique) and some small steamers. A soldier caustically described them as 'an assortment of scarcely seaworthy Greek coasting tramps and some larger rusty "death traps"'.[17] Escorted by Italian light destroyers, the ships were to travel in two flotillas, one sailing towards the beaches at Maleme and the other for Heraklion.

The caiques, powered largely by sails plus a weak engine, were very slow, so the initial flotilla set off on the evening of 19 May, heading first for the island of Milos. The plan was for the vessels to sail from Milos to Maleme during the day, when they would be under the cover of the Luftwaffe, but contradictory orders and poor

Right: German soldiers on a caique. [War Museum, Canea]

Above: One of the Italian destroyers escorting the invasion flotillas. [ATL: DA-01308]

winds meant that they and the second flotilla were still at sea heading for Crete when night fell on 21 May.

Admiral Cunningham knew about the German plans from Ultra intercepts, but he also sent an aircraft to 'locate' one of the flotillas. He had assembled a large part of the Mediterranean fleet in the waters around Crete and, while they were safe at night, they were very vulnerable to air attacks during the day. It was a great risk, but one he was willing to take in order to support Freyberg and thwart the sea invasion.

Around 11 p.m. an overwhelming force, three cruisers and four destroyers, intercepted the first flotilla some 20 kilometres off Crete. As the naval searchlights flashed on, the Italian destroyer bravely tried to protect her charges, but she was soon badly damaged by British shells and had to retire. The Royal Navy now turned murderous fire on the unarmed caiques, as one German soldier described:

> The ship's sails stand out white like a magnesium torch lit up by a beam from a searchlight . . . A fresh hit sets the ship alight. Some men are flung overboard by a blast from the detonation. Some had already jumped. They managed to reach a lifeboat and two dinghies. The ship sinks with a huge tongue of flame.[18]

The caiques scattered but, chased by the destroyers, were hunted down over two desperate hours. Around 320 troops were killed (as were some Greeks sailors pressed into manning the vessels), although others were later picked up by German

Right: Depth charges explode on a Royal Navy destroyer after an attack by the Luftwaffe in the seas off Crete. Despite this, the ship survived and limped back to Alexandria.

[ATL: DA-11867]

vessels and seaplanes. The British had offered no quarter, perhaps because of the casualties inflicted by the Luftwaffe on sailors, soldiers and civilians during the evacuation from Greece a month before. The German commanders were angered and Major General Ringel 'later argued that the enemy had fought unfairly, committing what amounted to war crimes'.[19]

The next morning was the second flotilla's turn when a section of it was intercepted by other ships of the Royal Navy. An Australian sailor on one of the cruisers recalled the slaughter:

> All ships switched on their searchlights and opened fire. It was a horrible massacre of defenceless men and boats, it had to be done. Soldiers jumped overboard and others were blown to kingdom come by murderous gunfire. The destroyers raced across the area churning the sea into a cauldron. It was soon over and once more the ocean was strewn with burning debris, patches of oil and dead men . . . war is inhuman and when a man has seen his comrades killed before his eyes he is apt to let instinct overcome reason.[20]

The remaining caiques returned to Piraeus and the Germans would send no more troops by sea until the airborne forces were sure of victory on Crete. Before this eventuated, however, the Luftwaffe took a dreadful revenge on the Royal Navy. From 8.30 a.m. on 22 May bombers carried out a relentless attack, damaging or sinking warships in the waters around Crete and then attacking the vessels sent to their aid. By the end of the day two cruisers and a destroyer were sunk and several other ships were badly damaged. One of the sailors described his ordeal after his cruiser, HMS *Fiji*, slid under the waves:

> I had to keep swimming. I was in there for I suppose just about six hours. Oh, it was very cold. That's what killed a lot of the men. We swam around there and I saw a lot of my friends die . . . It was just after midnight, I suppose, when we saw these two black shapes, destroyers . . . They came in and they pulled all these nets at the side, and picked us up. My tongue was hanging out there, solid salt.[21]

The same night five destroyers in a squadron captained by Lord Louis Mountbatten, which had been sent from Malta to patrol north of Crete, attacked some caiques and shelled Maleme airfield. The next morning, however, three of the destroyers were caught by dive bombers and two were soon sunk.

The loss of men and ships on 22 and 23 May was a terrible blow for the Mediterranean fleet. Cunningham concluded that any further losses would 'cripple the fleet', that 'sea control in the eastern Mediterranean could not be retained after such an experience' and that the navy, therefore, could no longer try to prevent seaborne attacks on Crete.[22] Fortunately for Freyberg, the Germans were not aware of this drastic decision.

To go back, then, to Crete and the night of 21 May: Freyberg and his staff, alerted by radio intercepts from a unit at Creforce headquarters, had gathered on a knoll to await the navy's attack on the first invasion flotilla. Geoffrey Cox later wrote that around 11.30 p.m., 'on the horizon away to the north came the flash and thunder of guns, and then the dull red glow of burning vessels'. Further intercepts confirmed that the German vessels either had been sunk or had fled. Cox then heard Freyberg say:

> 'It has been a great responsibility. A great responsibility.' His tones conveyed the deep thankfulness of a man who had discharged well a nightmarishly difficult task. His comment indicated, I believe, that he felt now the island was reasonably safe. He had reason to do so. The seaborne attack had been routed. At neither Retimo or Heraklion had the Germans secured a grip on an airfield. At Maleme . . . a counter-attack in substantial force . . . was about to go in. It seemed that we had turned the corner.[23]

But what Freyberg, Cox and the others on the knoll did not know was that the counter-attack at Maleme was already running late and that this delay would be the fatal blow to its chances of success.

Below: Servicing a 'pom pom' gun, one of the main anti-aircraft defences on the Royal Navy's ships.
[ATL: DA-01884]

1941
21 MAY
MIDNIGHT   Maori Battalion on the start line
22 MAY

3.30 A.M.   Counter-attack at Maleme begins

NOON

5 P.M.   Second counter-attack conference

8 P.M.   Ringel arrives on Crete

22 MAY
MIDNIGHT
23 MAY

King George II evacuated from Greece

5th Brigade withdraws from the Maleme sector

NOON

7

TOO LITTLE,
TOO LATE

In the early evening of 21 May a conference was held at Brigadier Hargest's headquarters to work out the details of the counter-attack to retake Maleme airfield and Point 107. Hargest's optimism of the previous day had evaporated and he seemed on the point of collapse.

Two New Zealand officers later said that the brigadier was so exhausted, he 'was unable to think coherently' and 'could not complete one sentence at a time'.[1] An account from British tank commander Roy Farran, who saw Hargest soon after, supports their views:

> He was a red, open-faced man, who looked like a country farmer and it was obvious that he was suffering from acute fatigue. He asked us to wait for half an hour while he had some sleep. Disgusted, intolerant, we sat on the steps until he was ready.[2]

Previous page: German reinforcements on a Greek airfield.
[ATL: Detail of DA-01312]

Below: Maori soldiers who fought on Crete.
[ATL: DA-06839]

Hargest had gone through a couple of stressful days and one night of disrupted sleep, but so had the other Allied commanders and they were not showing a similar level of exhaustion (although some would a week later). It is not unreasonable to assume that the bombing and strafing had brought on the symptoms of shell shock again, and his erratic and negative behaviour on this and the next day would appear to confirm this.

In any event, the conference was able to agree on a straightforward plan of attack. Farran's three light tanks were to move along the road leading to the airfield, with the 28th Maori Battalion on their left heading towards Point 107 and the Tavronitis River, while the 20th Battalion on the right would push forward to the airstrip. The start time for the advance was set at 1 a.m., as it was felt this would allow plenty of time for the 20th Battalion to arrive from its positions near Canea.

Hargest had not invited the commanders of the 21st and 23rd battalions to the conference. However, a role was found for the half-strength 21st Battalion, to attack towards the Tavronitis River on the southern side of Point 107. But the strong 23rd Battalion, which so far had suffered minimal casualties, was again held back with only a mopping-up task.

The Maori soldiers were on their start line by midnight and settled down across from the tanks to wait for their comrades from the 20th. However, the movement

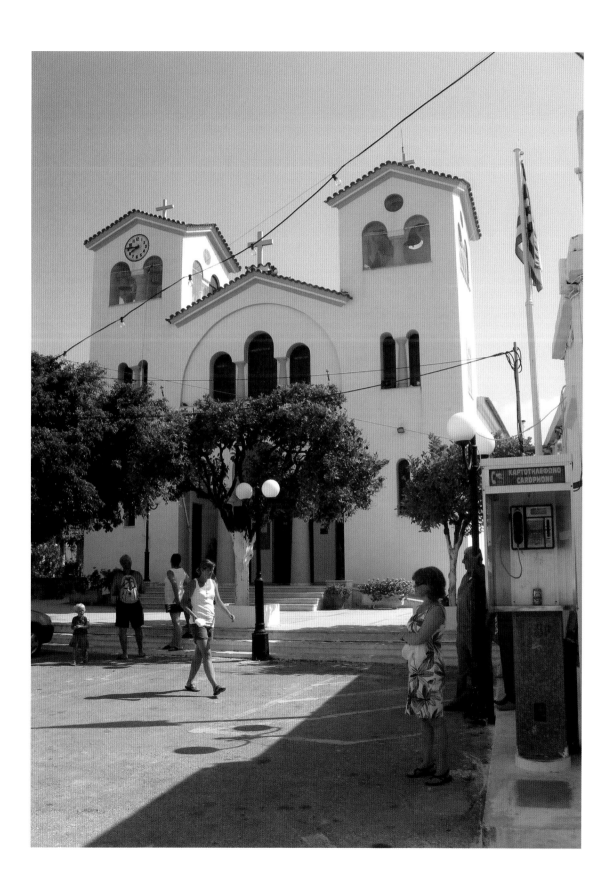

Previous page: The church in the square at Galatas. *[David Filer]*

Above left: The view across the now built-up land towards Maleme, from the hill above Platanias. *[David Filer]*

Left: Point 107 from the Tavronitis River. *[David Filer]*

Above: Maleme airfield from Point 107. *[David Filer]*

Right: The ridge behind Point 107, held by B Company, 22nd Battalion. *[David Filer]*

OBERGEFREITER
ANTON BRANDHOFER
31.1.1919 + 22.5.1941

OBERGEFREITER
KARL REICHER
30.10.1917 + 22.5.1941

209   210

Above: The German cemetery on Point 107.
[David Filer]

Left: The grave of two Germans killed during the battle. *[David Filer]*

Above right: New Zealand graves at Suda Bay. *[David Filer]*

Right: The Commonwealth War Graves Commission cemetery at Suda Bay.
[David Filer]

Left: A Cretan war memorial in the Prison Valley. [David Filer]

Right: A monument to a German airborne battalion, erected outside Canea during the war and now damaged and neglected. [David Filer]

Below: The memorial at Kondomari to the villagers massacred by German paratroopers in June 1941. [David Filer]

Above: Galatas Hill from the Prison Valley.
[David Filer]

Right: The road in Galatas up which the New Zealanders charged. *[David Filer]*

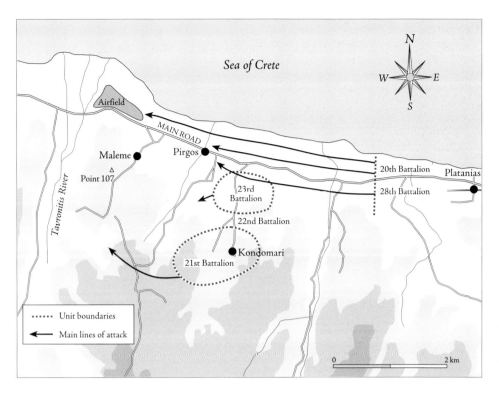

Map: The counter-attack at Maleme.

Below: Hargest at Platanias. [ATL: DA-12182]

of the 2/7th Battalion from Georgeoupolis and its changeover with the Kiwis had gone badly awry and, although trucks had picked up the Australians on time, they were bombed and strafed on the road, with constant hold-ups and the battalion being split. There were further delays passing through Canea and the first two companies did not approach the 20th Battalion's positions until around midnight. Everyone could see the gun flashes and fires out to sea and assumed that the navy had intercepted the German invasion fleet. The commander of the 20th, Major Jim Burrows, pressed Brigadier Puttick to allow his battalion to leave before the Australians arrived, but Puttick held firmly to Freyberg's instructions to wait for the relief force. Rumours of beach landings appeared to confirm this stance.

Once the first Australian companies had taken over some of the 20th's positions, Burrows set out for Platanias, ordering his men to follow as quickly as possible. However, it took some time to move out of the positions at night, load the vehicles and drive to Platanias, and it was 2.45 a.m. before the trucks carrying the first two of his companies arrived. Hargest by now had cold feet about the entire plan and asked Puttick if the counter-attack had to go ahead — the reply was, 'it must'.

At around 3.30 a.m., two and a half hours late, the Kiwis and the tanks moved forward. The men from the 20th soon found that the Germans were defending a series of pockets, rather than a fixed line. Charles Upham, who was taking the initial step in a series of remarkable actions that would win his first Victoria Cross, later wrote:

> Went on meeting resistance in depth — in ditches, behind hedges, in the top
> and bottom stories of village buildings, fields and gardens on road beside drome.
> The wire of 5 Bde [5th Brigade] hindered our advance. There were also mines
> and booby traps which got a few of us . . . There was T.G. [Tommy gun] and
> pistol fire and plenty of grenades and a lot of bayonet work which you don't often
> get in war . . . We had heavy casualties but the Germans had much heavier. They
> were unprepared. Some were without trousers, some had no boots on.[3]

One company of the 20th got up to the edge of the airfield, but it had suffered
many casualties and came under intense mortar and machine-gun fire. Burrows,
deciding that his men could go no further and it would be better if they tried to
support the Maori attack on Point 107, pulled his companies back to the south of
the road.

Initially, the 28th Battalion's advance had been easier, but night attacks had their
own problems, as one Maori officer, Ben Porter, recalled:

> We knew there was somebody crawling through the wheat, and I suspected it
> was our company commander's runner, bringing a message back. He stood up,
> about two yards in front of one of my boys, and of course everyone was a bit
> jittery . . . all he did was squeeze the trigger when this chap stood up in front of
> us, and shot him dead. So we never got any messages either, of course, because
> of that.[4]

As dawn approached, the Maori soldiers ran into increasing opposition, with heavy
fire from prepared German defences. Bayonet charges overcame some enemy posts
but, as one officer, wrote, 'there seemed to be German machine guns behind all the
trees'.[5] Meanwhile, Farran's three tanks had run into trouble, with the Germans
using British anti-aircraft guns captured at the airfield as anti-tank weapons. The
lead tank was hit and caught fire, another was damaged and the third was told not
to advance by itself. Their part in the
battle was at an end.

Below: Troops on the move in the Maleme sector. [ATL: DA-03466]

The 21st Battalion attacked in daylight
to the south and made rapid progress,
reaching a forward position they had
held two days before, overlooking
the Tavronitis River. Once again, this
battalion had more than made up for its
problems in the earlier Greek campaign.
However, as the day advanced, all the
New Zealand units faced increasing air
raids from the Luftwaffe. With constant
attack from the air and machine-gun
and mortar fire on the ground, the Kiwi
advance came to a standstill. The men

THE ESCAPE OF THE KING OF GREECE

Following the defeat of the Allies on Greece, King George II, other members of the royal family, the new prime minister and various hangers-on escaped to Crete, where they initially set up court in a villa at the ancient Minoan palace of Knossos. Some of the royal family, along with George's mistress, soon went to Cairo by flying boat, but the king and prime minister chose to stay on the island. They moved to a country house near Canea, which had recently been promoted to the new capital of 'free' Greece.

Freyberg wanted the king and his companions to depart for Cairo because he had much greater concerns than worrying about some prominent civilians, particularly once the paratroopers arrived. But Wavell, the British War Cabinet and the Foreign Office felt the king should remain on Greek soil, however limited, and so he stayed.

Just before the invasion a platoon of New Zealanders (from the 18th Battalion) and some armed Cretans were designated as the escort for the royal party and an evacuation plan was drawn up. On 20 May, however, after paratroopers landed less than a kilometre from the country house the royal party were staying in, there was a hasty departure for the mountains to the south. With the Kiwis forming a cordon, the royal party made hot work of the climb into the steep foothills. They were fired on by some Greek soldiers (who mistook them for Germans) and observed by enemy aircraft, but eventually reached a village where they could settle down for the night.

Freyberg now had to convince Middle East Command that the royal party (and another group from the British Legation) should be evacuated from the south coast. After some reluctance from the Cairo bureaucrats and more anxious messages from the general, it was agreed that both parties would be collected on the night of 22/23 May.

Once a British colonel who was travelling with the king was able to confirm that the Royal Navy would pick up the party near the village of Ay Roumeli on the coast, the civilians and soldiers continued their difficult climb through the mountains. The colonel later complimented the Kiwis, who were carrying weapons, ammunitions and supplies, for their patient perseverance.[6]

On 22 May, an equally hard descent to the south coast began. Some of the Kiwis and Greek troops went back to the north with the mules and donkeys, while the rest of the group slithered and clambered their way down to a settlement near the sea. Then, after trekking along a stream bed through a ravine, they met the legation party at Ay Roumeli.

After worrying hold-ups, the destroyer HMS *Decoy* was located off the coast in the middle of the night and the king, along with various officers, diplomats and politicians, was embarked. A decision was made to also take the Kiwi soldiers, rather than leave them at the south coast or send them back on an arduous march across the mountains.

Throughout the three-day ordeal all the soldiers and civilians had retained their respect for the king who, as the Greek prime minister said, 'with a majestic simplicity . . . shared with us all dangers, all privations, all hardships'.[7]

Above: Peter McIntyre, HM King George II of the Hellenes. [Archives New Zealand, AAAC 898 NCWA 271]

GEORGE II

sought cover and went to ground, and the counter-attack halted with none of the key objectives taken. In later years many veterans would argue that if they had left the start line on time and carried the attack forward during the hours of darkness, it would have been a different story.

By late morning, Hargest, who had received only limited information, had oddly reverted to a more optimistic mood. Out of touch with the front line, he informed divisional headquarters that progress was still being made and that his men now held the eastern side of the airfield. He even suggested that the Germans might be evacuating their forces, stating: 'Steady flow of enemy planes landing and taking off. May be trying to take troops off. Investigating.'[8] In fact, the Germans were bringing in more men and equipment and Hargest's own troops were withdrawing from the airfield. By the middle of the afternoon most of the Kiwis were back within the defence lines that the 5th Brigade had held before the counter-attack began. There had been many casualties but, as Davin wrote, when darkness fell 'the newcomers of 20 and 28 Battalions [were] grimly solacing themselves for their own losses by the sight of all the enemy dead'.[9]

Once Creforce headquarters realised that the counter-attack had failed, Freyberg called a conference at 5 p.m. to plan for a further attack that night. Two battalions in the 4th Brigade (one New Zealand and one Australian) were available, as was a strong British battalion at Canea. Those of Hargest's units which were still up to it would also have to take part. Puttick was sent off to sort out the details with Inglis and Hargest, but he was soon told that other threats were developing. The paratroopers once again had made a push towards Galatas (although this was seen off by the Kiwis, supported by fierce attacks by Greeks and Cretans), and there were indications that enemy forces might try to cut the coast road, thereby isolating all the New Zealanders in the Maleme area.

When Puttick got though to Hargest at Platanias, the 5th Brigade commander was in a negative mood again, stating that 'his troops had been severely attacked, were considerably exhausted, and certainly not fit to make a further attack'.[10] No doubt Hargest was trying to protect his battered brigade, but equally his battalions were still ready and willing to fight, as they would show in the following days. His pessimism infected Puttick, however, who now had doubts about a further counter-attack and informed Freyberg, adding that the 5th Brigade should be withdrawn. Freyberg sent a senior staff officer to make the final decision with Puttick and, largely as a result of Hargest's concerns, they agreed that the brigade should pull back that night to Platanias.

Below: Major General Ringel decorating mountain troops in Crete. [ATL: DA-12642]

Freyberg knew that this withdrawal would almost certainly mean that the airfield would remain in German hands, and that further reinforcements would pour through it. Yet he did not countermand his subordinate commanders and order an all-out attack. As Ian Stewart has written, Freyberg could have decided to have 'gone himself with his reserves along the open coast road . . . staking everything upon a final effort to drive back onto Hill 107, and so perhaps achieving a triumph that would have outdone all the exploits of his youth'.[11]

Instead, the fire-eater of the First World War chose caution. He must have known that if he sent all his reserves in an attack to seize Maleme airfield and it was unsuccessful, he would have nothing left to hold off any subsequent German assault. A general like Student might have taken the risk, but Freyberg was unwilling to stake everything on a single throw of the dice. He was probably right: the German force around Maleme had doubled in strength during the day and was already pushing forward. It would have been a tough ask to retake the airfield, but the decision to withdraw the New Zealanders meant that from this point on Creforce was on the back foot.

Freyberg now pinned his hopes on establishing a 'secure defence', by forming a line west and south of Galatas, which would allow the Allies to continue to hold the ports at Suda Bay and Canea. But it was impossible to stretch this line far enough to prevent the ever-increasing German forces from eventually outflanking it.

Throughout the third day of the conflict hundreds of transport planes had landed at Maleme airfield, bringing in around 2,000 fresh troops, plus ammunition and other supplies.

Major General Ringel of the 5th Mountain Division arrived in the evening and took command of all the German units on Crete. He formed three battle groups: the first would protect the airfield to the west and south and open up the small port at Kastelli Kisamou; the second would bring the surviving paratroopers together and move east along the coast; and the third and strongest group (three battalions of mountain troops) would thrust eastwards on an inland route. Its initial aims were to cut the coast road and link up with the airborne troops in Prison Valley. A day later the junction was achieved, much to the relief of the isolated paratroopers, as Captain von der Heydte recalled:

> I was almost certain that we couldn't win, because we had been hungry and thirsty and to the limit of our strength. And at this moment suddenly a lieutenant of the mountain troops came to my post of command, which was on a hill, and it was for us, I should say, an appearance of heaven, a gift from heaven.[12]

On 24 May a further 3,000 soldiers were flown into Maleme, and another group of mountain troops began to move south, to try to encircle the embattled Allies. Now the pendulum had clearly swung the Germans' way.

1941
23 MAY
MIDNIGHT
24 MAY

5th Brigade withdraws east of Galatas

Canea heavily bombed

24 MAY
MIDNIGHT
25 MAY

Student lands at Maleme

Galatas defence line collapses
Counter-attack at Galatas

25 MAY
MIDNIGHT
26 MAY

New Zealanders withdraw from the Galatas line

26 MAY
MIDNIGHT
27 MAY

Anzacs withdraw to Suda Bay positions

Force Reserve destroyed
Charge at 42nd Street

Wavell orders the evacuation of Crete

27 MAY
MIDNIGHT
28 MAY

8

A FIGHTING
WITHDRAWAL

The decision to withdraw the 5th Brigade and other New Zealand units in the western defence sector surprised the battalion commanders; as Lieutenant Colonel Leckie later wrote, 'all were of the opinion that we could hold the position'.[1] According to Second Lieutenant Thomas, the men were equally disgruntled:

> They had seen so many of the enemy dead that their morale was quite unshaken by the terrific air attacks by day. Man for man they considered that they could lick the German despite his superior weapons and equipment . . . [They] felt sullenly critical of the powers that were withdrawing them.[2]

However, after dawn on 23 May the Kiwis pulled back to positions around Platanias, with the Maori battalion pugnaciously performing the crucial role of rearguard. Some of the wounded who could not be moved remained with their medical officers and orderlies to become prisoners of war and most of the artillery had to be abandoned. As a result, Maleme airfield was no longer under the direct fire of the New Zealand gunners.

The Germans rapidly followed up the withdrawal and, even in its new positions, the 5th Brigade was soon threatened by mountain troops making an outflanking advance across the hills. Freyberg and Puttick decided that another move was needed and that night the brigade retired through the Kiwi lines west of Galatas. In less than 24 hours it had retreated more than twelve kilometres, moving into a reserve position in what would prove to be only a brief respite.

The key action now shifted to Galatas and the hills around it. The 4th Brigade, led by Brigadier Inglis, took overall responsibility for the sector and Kippenberger's worn-down 10th Brigade came under his command (and soon would cease to exist). However, after three days of fighting 'Kip' knew the Galatas area intimately, and because of this he remained in charge of the troops in that line. Defending the eastern flank of the sector were two Australian battalions (under Brigadier Vasey) and a Greek regiment.

As their foot soldiers moved up, the German air offensive intensified. On 24 May Canea was heavily bombed, both to disrupt military communications and to terrorise the Cretans and punish them for their resistance. (Heraklion was similarly bombed the following day.) Cox watched Canea 'disappear into a cloud of smoke, in the midst of which red flames twisted and leapt' and Hargest wrote that it was 'transformed from a pleasant little town to a smouldering dust heap with fires burning but otherwise dead'.[3]

Many civilians fled from Canea, but the soldiers had to hold their ground and cope with the incessant air attacks as best they could. The defences around Galatas were systematically bombed and, as the men crouched in their trenches, some felt that stress and fear would overwhelm them. One Kiwi wrote in his diary on 24 May:

Previous page: A German machine gunner overlooking the Gulf of Canea.

[ATL: DA-12643]

> Just a hell of a day. Worst to date. Machine-gunned and bombed mercilessly all day. Just lay in our slit trenches and hoped for the best. Have eaten nothing for three days. Stomach playing up.[4]

F reyberg was aware that the aerial assault was gradually grinding down his men. He signalled Wavell that the Luftwaffe's attack 'has been savage', that his men were 'very tired' and that 'anything you can do to neutralise the air situation would help us materially'.[5] Middle East Command did what it could within its widely stretched resources. A squadron of Hurricanes was sent from Egypt to Heraklion on 23 May but, after a series of mishaps, only one arrived. However, more Hurricanes landed later and another group attacked German positions around the city. Also, for four nights in a row RAF bombers raided Maleme airfield and its surrounds.

Further support came in the form of some army and commando reinforcements that Wavell located and despatched. Unfortunately, because of the threat of air attacks the ships carrying the soldiers did not reach Crete and had to return to Alexandria, but 500 commandos, led by Colonel Laycock, did arrive at Suda Bay on the nights of 24 and 26 May. Among them was the author Evelyn Waugh, who would later write, in his novel *Officers and Gentlemen*, an acerbic account of the last days on Crete.

On Sunday 25 May, as Wavell and Freyberg were trying to shore up the defences, General Student landed on Crete. His arrival showed that the Germans believed that victory was in their grasp, even though his Parachute Division had suffered terrible casualties, many of whom were lying rotting in the olive groves near by. The sense of victory was enhanced when, on the same day, the Nazi hierarchy finally allowed Radio Berlin to announce that German forces had invaded the island. But the men on the ground knew that, despite some success, more hard fighting was still to come.

Above: Kiwi soldiers rest by a road west of Canea. [Filer collection]

Throughout that Sunday the German units built up along the two-kilometre front running south and west around Galatas and through the line of hills leading to the sea. In the afternoon, as dive bombing, machine gunning and mortar fire reached a crescendo, the mountain troops and paratroops attacked. A German war correspondent described the advance:

> It is bound to be hard going. The British are thoroughly aware that the Galatas heights are worth a capital city. Once again we have to fight our way through this wretched olive grove. Dense cactus woods and agave thickets shove themselves forward forming wide barriers covering the whole terrain and closing off the view of everything lying ahead.[6]

The camouflage and intense fire soon helped the Germans close up to the long western defence line held by the 18th Battalion. After hand-to-hand combat and a ragged counter-attack failed to stop the advance, some men in the battalion surrendered, while others fell back in disarray, as their war history relates:

> For a few minutes all order was lost, the men streaming back with Jerry [the Germans] right on their heels firing everything he had. They dumped everything except rifles and ammunition. They ran as they had never believed they could. Back down Murray Hill and up to the next ridge, where Colonel Gray was shouting, swearing, rallying all comers to make a stand. The most resolute stopped there, lined a stone wall with rifles and Tommy guns, and held Jerry off for a few more minutes . . . Then once more streams of fire came in from the flank as Jerry poured into Galatas and back again the line had to go, every man for himself.[7]

Below: Mountain troops advancing in Crete. [ATL: DA-12651]

The Composite Battalion, the scratch infantry unit which had been formed from gunners and drivers to defend the hills around Galatas, had fought well for several days but now also disintegrated. Standing outside Galatas, Kippenberger knew that the critical moment of the battle had arrived. He threw his only reserves into the crumbling front and urged Inglis to send reinforcements. The brigadier found some signallers from his headquarters and sent them forward as infantry, along with the Brigade Band and the Kiwi Concert Party. They joined the firing line, while the 23rd Battalion moved quickly up from the 5th Brigade's reserve positions along the road to Canea.

Kippenberger, however, was now surrounded by a stream of panicked

retreating men. As their retreat threatened to become a rout, he walked among them, yelling, 'Stand for New Zealand! Stand every man who is a soldier!'[8] This dramatic (and now famous) gesture worked: the men paused, allowed themselves to be formed into sections and were despatched to establish a new defence line.

By early evening, however, the Kiwis who had fought bravely south of Galatas had also been forced to withdraw and the Germans had occupied the village. But the arrival of the 23rd Battalion along with two light tanks under Roy Farran gave Kippenberger the chance to retake this important position. He decided that 'it was no use trying to patch the line any more: obviously we must hit or everything would crumble away'.[9] With the tanks in front, the soldiers of the 23rd fixed bayonets and prepared to attack. Men from other units came forward to join them. Just after 8 p.m. the tanks set off, followed by the charging Kiwis, who 'broke spontaneously into the most blood curdling of shouts and battle cries', their yells combining in a terrifying 'deep throated wild-beast noise'.[10]

The soldiers charged up the narrow road towards the square with the Germans firing from the houses and throwing grenades. The New Zealanders shot back, then closed in horrifying hand-to-hand fighting: Lieutenant Thomas later wrote how bayonets entered 'throats and chests with . . . hesitant ease'[11] and a fellow officer recalled a fight to the death in the square:

Above: New Zealand gunners on Crete.
[ATL: DA-11070]

Below: One of the tanks which took part in the battle for Galatas.
[ATL: DA-12645]

The German had Larsen by the throat at arm's length while he fumbled with his other hand for a knife. Kennedy and I had rifles with bayonets and as we hopped in, the 'Hun' used Larsen as a shield to keep us off. As we separated to get around him, he exposed his back for a moment and Kennedy split his head with a lovely butt stroke. Larsen was a man with a grown family but was up and off in the hunt in no time.[12]

The ferocious attack broke the Germans' spirit and their remaining men abandoned the village. There were many casualties, including some Cretans sheltering in their cellars, and the two tanks were destroyed. Both Farran and Thomas received severe wounds and were later taken prisoner. (In Greece, after they had recovered, they would make separate ingenious escapes and eventually reach Allied lines.)

Although the New Zealanders had retaken Galatas, their commanders knew it was only a brief respite. Puttick decided that a shorter defence line was needed, running from the Australian positions (which were to the east of Galatas) to the sea. At 4th Brigade headquarters Inglis suggested a counter-attack, but there were not enough fresh troops available. He then accepted that Galatas could not be held and during the night the Kiwis pulled back to the new line. Next morning the Germans cautiously reoccupied the battered village.

The Allied defences were now only a kilometre from the outskirts of Canea. In the north were the New Zealanders of the 5th Brigade (plus the 19th Battalion and some other Kiwis drafted into the infantry) led by Hargest, below them were the Australians under Vasey, and a Greek regiment held the hills further south. Freyberg now decided to form a new brigade out of 1,200 British troops around Canea, centred on the still strong 1st Welsh Regiment. He put Inglis in charge of this 'Force Reserve', which was to replace the Kiwis in their front-line positions on the night of 26 May.

Freyberg also decided that Major General Weston would leave his Suda Bay base and take command of the forward area, including the New Zealand Division. It was a confusing reshuffle and, with officers becoming increasingly stressed and tired, a recipe for the disaster that followed. At a meeting the British general was 'short' with Inglis, who got the impression that Weston 'intended to use these troops [Force Reserve] himself and not through me'.[13] It is possible that Weston by now had some doubts about the Kiwis' abilities, particularly after his experience that day with a couple of Maori soldiers:

Below: The church at Galatas, after the battle (with two German graves in front).

[ATL: DA-12653]

The pair had distinguished themselves by capturing an English general, who had not appeared to relish being bailed up by a couple of tough-looking Maoris and made to identify himself. The name of General Weston meant nothing to them at the time, but his promise that they would hear more of it at a later date was not very reassuring. In actual fact, the Royal Marines were nearly deprived of a general for he was a little slow in putting his hands up.[14]

Above: A German soldier moves cautiously into Galatas on the morning after the battle. The bodies of men killed in the fighting lie along the road. [ATL: DA-12652]

Throughout 26 May the Germans pressed hard against the Kiwis and Aussies in their new line, penetrating the flanks at either end. Hargest and Vasey, feeling that their defences would soon be broken, told Puttick that they should all withdraw that night to positions further east. Because there were no phone or wireless links, Puttick had to walk several kilometres to take their concerns to Freyberg (who had spent much of the day zooming around key positions on the back of a motorcycle). But the general was preoccupied with bigger issues; he had to keep the Germans back from Suda Bay so that desperately needed food, ammunition and reinforcements could be landed. He bluntly told Puttick that the men must hold their ground.

Soon after Puttick and Vasey repeated the request to withdraw to Weston, who said Freyberg would have to be consulted again. It took some hours before Weston found the Creforce commander, who insisted again that the line be held, and more precious time passed before a despatch rider got this message to Puttick. In the interim, however, the New Zealand brigadier had decided to withdraw 'with or

Above: German troops advance through Galatas. [ATL: DA-12649]

without orders' and soon the Kiwis and Aussies were scampering back to new positions near Suda Bay.[15] Tired and under pressure, Puttick had succumbed to the demands of Vasey and Hargest. With surprising decisiveness, this old-school Regular officer had disobeyed his commanding general and shown an uncharacteristic and dangerous independence. A disaster would quickly follow.

Weston had already sent the newly formed Force Reserve forward to take over the New Zealand defence line. The British soldiers arrived in the middle of the night to find no one there but, following Weston's orders, occupied the position. They did not know that, with the Australians also gone, their southern flank was now totally exposed. Unfortunately, Inglis, who could have told them this, had, instead of taking command of Force Reserve, stayed put at the headquarters of the New Zealand Division. Ian Stewart, who served with the 1st Welsh, was later highly critical of Inglis' decision, suggesting ambition lay behind it:

> Not without reason, he [Inglis] believed that promotion might soon afford him more scope to exercise those talents of which he was confidently aware. In sombre contrast with such hopes there had come to him out of the blue this totally unexpected commission offering little more than the probability of death or capture upon a forlorn venture among strangers.[16]

Certainly, on the morning of 27 May, death or capture seemed the fate awaiting the men of Force Reserve. An overwhelming army of German airborne and mountain troops, backed by guns and aircraft, attacked head on, while other paratroopers stormed around the open flank and encircled the British soldiers. Some of them fought their way out, but most were killed or taken prisoner. As Beevor has commented, 'this sorry blunder had thrown away nearly a thousand of the fittest troops left', men who might have been used much more effectively days earlier in a counter-attack at Maleme.[17]

An already exhausted Weston was shattered by this debacle. As he and his staff pulled back well beyond Suda Bay, he told two New Zealand battalion commanders 'that they were fools to stay where they were', and when he met Freyberg he blurted out 'we must capitulate and all surrender'.[18] But Freyberg was made of sterner stuff: he knew he had to try to hold a line and preserve as much of his force as possible.

The New Zealand and Australian troops had now taken up positions south of Suda Bay along a rough road leading into the foothills, which the soldiers called '42nd Street' (because the 42nd Field Company had earlier been stationed there). An inexperienced and overly confident German battalion closed up to the line. The Kiwis and Aussies, frustrated by so many withdrawals, decided to hit the enemy hard, as a battalion war history relates:

> A runner from the Australians reported to Major Royal (28 Battalion) his Colonel's compliments and asked what they were going to do about the advancing Germans. The runner was told that the Maoris were fed up with being pushed around and were going in with the bayonet . . . another message came from the Australians asking the Maoris to wait a little and the Australians would be pleased to join them. The forward companies of 21 Battalion had scarcely lined the sunken road when they heard yells that could come only from Maori throats. It was a blood-stirring haka. The Australians produced a scream even more spine-chilling than the Maori effort, and the sight of the Maori Battalion charging with vocal accompaniment sent the whole line surging forward.[19]

A young officer with the Maori Battalion, Rangi Logan, later recalled how the enemy were driven back:

> On and on they [the Maori] went among the trees, their yells getting further and further away. Meanwhile my platoon were reluctant to stop; they were steamed up and keen to keep going. Tainui and others had already found about a dozen Germans lying low in a ditch with a German shepherd dog: we had shot the lot and were looking for more . . . Eventually the boys came straggling back; their complaint was that the Germans wouldn't stand and fight, and those that weren't killed were too busy running hard to get away.[20]

The German battalion was destroyed and from then on their pursuing troops were more careful. The charge at 42nd Street was, however, a last hurrah for the Allies, as the end of the battle was fast approaching.

When the New Zealand troops withdrew from Galatas and the surrounding hills in the early hours of 26 May, Freyberg sensed that defeat was inevitable. The Germans would soon occupy the port of Canea and from there, would be able to fire on Suda Bay.

After nearly a week of fighting his soldiers were worn down and he had been informed that the Greek forces were on the point of disintegration. He concluded that the only sensible option was to try to evacuate as many of the men as possible. Following a conference around 9 a.m. he sent a cable to Middle East Command, stating:

Below: Paratroopers and mountain troops in the Cretan hills.
[ATL: DA-12650]

> I regret to have to report that in my opinion the troops under my command here at Suda Bay have reached the limit of endurance . . . from an administrative point of view the difficulties of extricating this force in full are now insuperable. A certain proportion of the force might be embarked provided a decision is reached at once . . . If, in view of the whole Middle East position, you decide that hours help, we will carry on.[21]

While waiting for Wavell's reply, Freyberg began planning the withdrawal of his force in the Suda Bay area to ports on the south coast of Crete. But Wavell, who knew that Churchill still had great hopes for a victory on the island, asked Freyberg to continue to hold on or to withdraw to Retimo and join up with the units there. Freyberg sent a blunt response:

> It is obvious that you do not realise the situation here. Retimo is practically foodless and without ammunition, and is cut off by road in every direction . . . Our only chance with the present force, which has been battered and shaken by an overwhelming air force, is to hide by day and return by night to selected beaches . . . I urge, therefore, that the only course is to go to Sphakia, which seems to give some chance of saving some of my force.[22]

This time Wavell got the message, and on the morning of 27 May informed Churchill that Crete could no longer be held and the troops would have to be withdrawn. After waiting for six hours without a reply, Wavell made the decision himself and ordered the evacuation of the island. Eventually, London sent its agreement and the Royal Navy was once again told to prepare to save as many men as possible from a defeated British army.

Below: A Maori soldier with his rifle and bayonet (Egypt, 1942).
[ATL: DA-02564]

1941

27 MAY
MIDNIGHT
28 MAY
Freyberg withdraws to Sfakia

Battle of Stilos

28 MAY
MIDNIGHT
29 MAY
Evacuation of Heraklion
Evacuation begins at Sfakia

29 MAY
MIDNIGHT
30 MAY
Second night of evacuation at Sfakia

Surrender at Retimo

30 MAY
MIDNIGHT
31 MAY
Third night of evacuation at Sfakia
Freyberg leaves Crete

31 MAY
MIDNIGHT
1 JUNE
Last night of evacuation at Sfakia

Surrender at Sfakia

9

HE WHO FIGHTS AND RUNS AWAY [1]

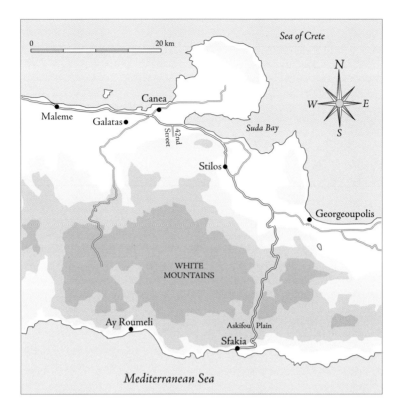

Previous page: Kiwi soldiers leave their trucks during the retreat. [Filer collection]

Map: The route to Sfakia.

With the evacuation finally approved, Freyberg decided to head south to the small coastal town of Sfakia to take charge of the operation. Brigadier Chappel at Heraklion was informed that the Royal Navy would take his troops off from that city's port on the night of 28 May, but it proved impossible to get a message through to Lieutenant Colonel Campbell at Retimo to tell him to move his men to the south coast.

Freyberg was worried that if a coded signal containing the evacuation plans was sent, the Germans might break it, radio links on the island were poor anyway, and attempts to inform Campbell by sea and air failed.

The withdrawal from the Suda Bay area was a complete shambles. Word had got round that an evacuation would occur from Sfakia, so most of the non-combat troops and other army, air force, naval and civilian stragglers immediately rushed towards the winding, narrow and unsealed road over the mountains. Some were on foot while the rest 'appropriated' any vehicles they could find. It was a 60-kilometre journey through the foothills, up into the White Mountains, across the high Askifou Plain and then down to where the road stopped on the cliff above Sfakia. Freyberg, who made the trip in 'a commandeered car which was already disintegrating owing to a bomb-torn radiator', later recalled the depressing sight of an army in retreat:

There were some units still sticking together and marching in order with their weapons, but in the main non-fighting troops in full flight — a disorganised rabble making its way doggedly and painfully to the south. There were thousands of unarmed troops including Cypriots and Palestinians. Without leadership, without any sort of discipline, it was impossible to expect anything else of troops who had not been trained as fighting soldiers.[2]

Fortunately, the fighting soldiers were still in action to the north, manning the last defences below Suda Bay and protecting the road through the hills. The newly arrived commandos had been given the role of rearguard, with the New Zealand 5th and the Australian 19th brigades holding the road below them. The 4th Brigade was sent back to guard the Askifou Plain (in case of a paratroop landing) and to hold its northern exit.

Despite Weston's pessimism, Freyberg had ordered him to take charge of the rear defences but, caught up in the chaotic retreat, he disappeared for half a day. Evelyn Waugh caustically said that Weston 'seemed to have lost his staff and his head' and Puttick, Hargest and Vasey had to act without him: as Puttick told Hargest, 'you are technically still under Gen Weston but he cannot be located'.[3] Hargest had no problem with this for he had shaken off his earlier inertia and it appears that any effects of shell shock had passed. In fact, as one battalion's war history indicates, Hargest was at his best during the last days on Crete:

> Brigadier Hargest urged all units to keep their men together, to adopt a reasonably easy pace, to conserve water and to retain arms and ammunition. His wise counsel was followed to the benefit of all and some stragglers were picked up. The Brigadier's determination to bring his brigade out as nearly intact as possible was a major factor in the success of this withdrawal.[4]

Below left: Pushing a truck off the road on the retreat to Sfakia.
[ATL: DA-12183]

Below: Hargest and his officers during their last days on Crete.
[ATL: DA-10349]

The enemy meantime continued to advance. Once the Force Reserve had been destroyed, the German troops had moved into the shattered town of Canea, with the paratroopers under Captain von der Heydte in the lead. He later described their careful progress to the town centre:

> It was an eerie feeling, making our way through the ruins towards our objective. The streets were strewn with debris, and here and there a fire still smouldered. The smell of oil and wine, so typical of any Greek town, mingled nauseatingly with the acrid stench of burning and the sweetish odour of decomposing bodies.[5]

The mayor surrendered what was left of the town to von der Heydte, who set up his headquarters in a large building overlooking the eastern beach which had previously housed the British Consulate (and is now the Hotel Doma).

With Canea taken and Suda Bay in his grasp, Major General Ringel now had to decide on his next course of action. Once again German intelligence and reconnaissance let its commanders down, so that Ringel was unaware that the bulk of Creforce was trying to escape via Sfakia. In any event he decided that relieving the beleaguered paratroopers at Retimo and Heraklion was his first priority. He ordered most of his force to advance along the road or through the hills towards Retimo, with only one regiment heading south. The paratroopers under his command were left to clear and hold the coastal area from Maleme to Suda Bay and soon saw German light tanks coming down the main road. They had been landed at the western port of Kastelli Kisamou, where fighting had finally ceased on 26 May, and were rolling along towards Retimo.

When the British and Australian troops at Heraklion learnt that they were to be evacuated on the night of 28 May, they were bewildered and disturbed.

Below left: Paratroopers enter a Cretan town. [War Museum, Canea]

Below right: German headquarters in Canea, photographed by one of their officers. [Hotel Doma, Canea]

Despite running short of food and ammunition, they had kept the Germans on the back foot for over a week (although paratroop reinforcements had recently arrived and some positions south of the airfield had been seized by the Germans). Now it seemed the Allies were to cut and run, leaving their brave Cretan friends to face the enemy's wrath alone.

Orders were orders, however, and Brigadier Chappel and his commanders quickly planned a careful withdrawal. At 9.30 p.m. the first companies began moving from the airfield to the harbour and the others steadily followed. Two hours later eight Royal Navy warships arrived off the coast and the destroyers began ferrying the waiting men out to the cruisers. Around 4,000 soldiers were embarked, along with a few Greeks and Cretans, and the ships were soon on their way to Egypt without the Germans on land even being aware of their departure.

But the Germans in the air were luckier. The damaged steering gear on one of the navy vessels jammed and her crew and soldiers had to be taken on board another destroyer. This in turn slowed down the entire flotilla which was then caught in daylight by the Luftwaffe. One Australian soldier described the terrifying experience of being on a ship under aerial assault:

> As soon as the plane appears overhead you can feel the boat lift out of the water as she puts on speed. Then the deck rolls over at an angle of 45 degrees. Then back it comes again and down goes the other side as she zigzags, turns and squirms at 40 knots, trying to spoil their aim. Down comes the Stuka and lets his bomb go . . . every gun is firing all the time and the noise is deafening. The six-inch and four-inch shake the whole boat and the multiple pom-pom is going like a steam-hammer. Four-barrelled multiple machine guns mounted on each side of the ship add to the general din.[6]

The Luftwaffe attacked the warships for six hours as they steamed towards Egypt. The destroyer *Hereward* was so badly hit that she had to turn back and be run

Below left: British troops evacuated from Heraklion. [E. Neville]

Below right: The badly damaged cruiser, HMS Orion, after the Crete campaign. [E. Neville]

aground on Crete (where most of those on board were eventually taken prisoner). Bombs struck the cruisers *Orion* and *Dido*; more than 650 men were killed or wounded, but the battered ships were able to eventually limp to safety. On this nightmare voyage many more soldiers from the garrison at Heraklion were lost than in their earlier fighting against the paratroops. Finally, on the evening of 29 May, the survivors reached the safety of Alexandria.

On the same evening as Heraklion was abandoned, the navy began the larger evacuation at Sfakia (which was to continue for three more nights). More than 200 walking-wounded, including some who had painfully struggled across the mountains, were taken on board four destroyers, along with some 800 coast defence and non-combat troops from the Suda area (to which HMAS *Napier* added three women, two children and a dog).[7] After this, most of the evacuees would be fighting men, including, it was hoped, the soldiers still holding off the Germans in the north.

A series of rearguard actions had already been fought on 28 May. Two companies of the Maori Battalion and some commandos briefly held a position near the turn-off from the main coast road, but they were soon surrounded by advancing Germans and the Maori soldiers had to carry out a difficult cross-country withdrawal.

Around the same time and a few kilometres south, the 5th Brigade was settling in about the village of Stilos for a much-needed daytime rest. Two officers from the 23rd Battalion decided on a brief reconnoitre before retiring, only to see a large party of Germans approaching from the west. The Kiwi soldiers were immediately roused and made a desperate race to reach a stone wall, gaining it just before the enemy arrived. Clive Hulme took the lead in the fire fight that followed:

> Hulme was among the first to arrive and opened fire from behind the stone wall just when the enemy leaders were about 15 yards away . . . After the leading elements . . . had been repelled, Hulme was to be seen sitting side-saddle on the stone wall, shooting at the enemy on the lower slopes. His example did much to maintain the morale of men whose reserves of nervous and physical energy were nearly exhausted.[8]

Despite this success, Hargest and Vasey realised that if a stronger German force appeared, their units were in danger of being surrounded. They took the difficult decision to make a daylight march to the south and risk attacks by the Luftwaffe. If the brigadiers had known that the German High Command had already begun withdrawing their squadrons in Greece to prepare for the attack on the Soviet Union, they would have felt more confident. In fact, their men were able to pull back without being bombed. Meanwhile the commandos and an Australian battalion, supported by a lone tank, held off another enemy attack along the road, before withdrawing during the night.

The fighting men now joined the stragglers and non-combat personnel on the

Above: New Zealand
troops pass a mountain
village, en route to the
south coast of Crete.

[A.R. Fitchett/Filer collection]

difficult march over the White Mountains. Although the distance along the road was
only 20 kilometres, it wound from 90 metres above sea level at Stilos to 900 metres
at the pass leading to the Askifou Plain. This climb was a terrible strain for tired
men, many still carrying their weapons and helping the wounded struggle on. As
Davin wrote, 'time and again the sight of a man stumbling along with an arm around
the neck of each of two comrades who took turns carrying his rifle stressed its echo
of Calvary'.[9]

The road was littered with wrecked vehicles and abandoned equipment and
personal items. There was little food and the wells along the route were often dry or
contaminated. Where water was found, there was chaos, as one Kiwi soldier recalled:

> Around this well were Greeks, Aussies, Tommies and N.Z ders all mad with thirst
> and I have never seen such a terrible and raving crazy mob. Rifle pullthroughs and
> anything in the shape of string were joined together to make a rope upon which
> tins, tin hats or anything that would hold water was tied and used to drag water
> from the well. As these were pulled up a hat would tip over only a foot from a
> reaching hand or a string would break.[10]

Although there were fewer enemy aircraft, the fear of strafing and bombing
remained, and most of the men slept in the day and moved at night. It was very
difficult to keep the exhausted soldiers moving, as Rangi Logan in the Maori
Battalion found:

> With darkness coming on, little food and after a hard day the men were moving automatically, almost insensible to time and place. It was then that I had the greatest difficulty in holding them together and keeping them moving. After the usual ten minutes halt the task would have been impossible without the assistance of men like Tainui, Matthews and several more of the really tough soldiers. As the night wore on kicks and swear words had to be used. Some of the men had almost given in and pleaded for 'Just another five minutes and I'll be OK' and 'I'll catch you up but just let me have a little sleep'.[11]

Within this relentless ordeal, however, there were some scenes of surreal humour that would briefly lift men's spirits. Geoffrey Cox saw a fetching blonde woman (a cabaret singer from Athens) in a khaki uniform along the road and Roy Ferguson remembered an Australian passing him on a donkey, calling 'Make way for the Australian Light Horse'.[12]

By the morning of 29 May the rearguard had struggled up to the northern exit of the high Askifou Plain, about ten kilometres from the south coast. The 23rd Battalion in the pass, with the Australian infantry in support, held off German attacks during the day, and both groups were later able to withdraw across the plain. That night eight Royal Navy warships arrived off Sfakia and 6,000 men were successfully embarked and taken back to Egypt. But the bulk of the fighting men — the 4th and 5th New Zealand brigades and the 19th Australian Brigade — were still awaiting their turn.

On 30 May Australian and British soldiers formed the rearguard on the southern side of the plain. When the German mountain troops were held along the road, their commander sent some men down the nearby ravines that led to the sea. According to Kippenberger, there was panic at Creforce headquarters as firing broke out when one party of Germans got close to the coast:

> At Sphakia when the Germans broke through almost to the beach, the General [Freyberg] & most others lost their heads and were dancing around giving orders to all & sundry. Inglis saw me and asked if I could do anything and I took my faithful 20th, what was left of them, told the General to keep quiet & fixed up the matter without any trouble.[13]

Above: A soldier fills his water bottle during the retreat. [ATL: DA-08185]

As one group of Kiwis blocked the ravine through which the Germans were descending, Charles Upham led his platoon up a steep hill above it and then killed the infiltrators by firing down upon them. This would be the final step in the actions that led to the award of his first Victoria Cross.

That night four destroyers were meant to arrive to take off the soldiers of the 4th and 5th brigades but, after the terrible casualties in the ships returning from Heraklion, Admiral Cunningham had decided to restrict the numbers of evacuees on board each vessel. So Freyberg had to make a tough decision; while most of the 4th Brigade could be embarked, the rest, along with the 5th Brigade, would have to wait another day. In any event, only two destroyers turned up, so they still ended

up packed to the gunnels with stressed but grateful men.

When the soldiers arrived at the beach, they found a cordon ringing the
embarkation point and holding back the increasingly anxious stragglers. Roy
Ferguson was part of the guard:

> We were told that if we let anybody through it would be possible that we'd be
> left behind . . . we had guys come along and told us they were diplomats, and
> they'd go away and come back as brigadiers and generals, and all sorts of things
> to try and get through the ring, and nobody got through to my knowledge.[14]

The next day the evacuees sailed into Alexandria to see a harbour full of wrecks.
A large part of the Mediterranean fleet had been sunk or damaged during the
operations to support Creforce, and Cunningham planned to send only four
destroyers for the final night of the evacuation. However, he reckoned without New
Zealand Prime Minister Peter Fraser.

Fraser had been in Egypt for two weeks and had already survived a nasty car
crash. On the road between Alexandria and Cairo, his vehicle had 'burst a tyre and
rolled over three or four times'.[15] With only a bump on his head he had carried on,
pressing Wavell and Churchill to provide more assistance to the forces on Crete.
Now he met Cunningham in Alexandria and doggedly reminded him that the Kiwis
still on the island made up a major part of the country's war effort. Cunningham
acknowledged this argument and agreed to send the cruiser *Phoebe* back with
four smaller vessels (with orders added to embark at least 3,500 men). These five

warships, later supported by two anti-aircraft cruisers (one of which was sunk), represented 'half the operational force left to the Mediterranean fleet' after the dreadful losses in the seas around Crete.[16]

✠ ✠ ✠

Major General Weston was now in command of what remained of Creforce, as Freyberg, under instruction from Wavell, had reluctantly left by flying boat on the night of 30 May. The weary and defeated Kiwi general later wrote:

> My feelings can be imagined better than described. I was handing over a difficult situation with the enemy through in one place almost to the beaches from which we were to make our last attempt to get away the remnants of the fighting force that still held out, tired, hungry and thirsty on the heights above.[17]

Fortunately for the Allies, the German commander just north of Sfakia had decided to postpone the encirclement of the rearguard and build up his forces before advancing to the coast on 2 June. The Allied troops would not have to fight their way to the embarkation point, but the question remained, who would get off and who would stay? The commandos had already been told that as the last into the battle, they would be the last fighting men off. Weston, Hargest and Vasey then made the hard decision that only the New Zealand and Australian brigades and some British soldiers and marines would definitely have a place in the boats.

On the evening of 31 May the Kiwi battalions that had fought so hard for eleven days moved steadily down to the beaches. Once again they formed a cordon to prevent the now desperate stragglers from rushing the boats, as the 21st Battalion war history describes:

Right: Admiral Cunningham and Prime Minister Fraser await the arrival of troops from Crete.

[ATL: Detail of DA-01176]

Far right: A soldier wounded on Crete is brought ashore in Alexandria.

[ATL: DA-01618]

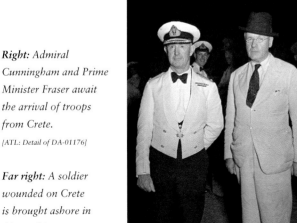

> They passed through a grim-faced cordon from 22 and 28 Battalions with rifles
> loaded and bayonets fixed, ready to use either bullet or steel on any stragglers
> who attempted to embark before the fighting men. Some had tried, but their fate
> convinced the mixed crowd of Greeks, Jews, Palestinians from labour units, as
> well as Australian, English, and New Zealand troops who had thrown away their
> arms, that the cordon meant to do the job it was there for.[18]

The sailors on the warships welcomed the weary men with buttered bread and hot
cocoa and crammed them into every space. As one Kiwi recalled: 'We were very
crowded, it was hot as a furnace. But it would not have mattered to us if the ship
had been a slave trader so glad were we to be off Crete.'[19]

Unfortunately, in the final chaotic hours one of the Australian battalions was left
behind (while some of the commandos, including their colonel, got off the island).
Weston left by flying boat and took Hargest with him. The following day the senior
officer remaining surrendered to the Germans. The shock to the more than 6,000
Allied men still on the south coast was enormous, as one Kiwi gunner later wrote:

> God Almighty! What a blow. A Prisoner of War. Me, I had had visions of wounds,
> death from various causes, including a fight to the finish in the event of a hand
> to hand go, but a prisoner, never. It was something that I had never reckoned on.
> The realisation was stupefying, dumbfounding.[20]

Below left: Freyberg in a cave at Sfakia, his final headquarters on Crete. [Sir John White]

Not all the soldiers left along the beaches were willing to go into captivity, however.
Some found abandoned landing craft and, using improvised sails after the fuel
ran out, crossed the Mediterranean to British lines. Others took to the hills where
the Cretans sheltered them, often for many months, until they were taken off by
caiques, submarines and naval patrol boats. Not all the adventurers got away;

Below right: Allied prisoners of war on Crete. [ATL: DA-03403]

many were eventually captured and met again in the prison camps the men who had surrendered immediately the battle was over.

The Australians at Retimo also ended up either surrendering or escaping. They were never informed about the evacuation plans and, although they ran short of supplies, continued to pressure the paratroopers through ten days of fighting. Then, on 29 May, German reinforcements were seen approaching and the next morning Lieutenant Colonel Campbell realised that Canea must be in enemy hands. Soon the Aussies were facing a powerful German force advancing from the west, including tanks and artillery. Campbell, a Regular officer, decided that there was no option but to surrender. However, the commander of the other battalion, Major Sandover, was a pre-war part-time soldier, and chose to give his men the option of surrendering or attempting to escape.

So one brave and resourceful officer went into captivity along with the remaining soldiers in his battalion, while the other took to the hills. Sandover eventually led 52 officers and men to the south coast where, after much help from the Cretans, they escaped by submarine to Egypt.

Having taken Retimo, the German forces continued their march to Heraklion and beyond. Isolated pockets of Cretan resistance were ruthlessly crushed. In the eastern arm of the island they linked up with some Italian forces which had landed at Sitia, with no opposition, on 28 May. Mussolini, having provoked war with Greece many months before, now wanted to be in on the final act.

Right: German artillery during the last days of fighting in northern Crete. [US National Archives, 242-GAP-157-C-4]

CASUALTIES OF THE BATTLE OF CRETE

And we who were there remember,
Those days of 'hell' on Crete,
And hope that when our time comes,
Those pals again we'll meet;
And as we trudge along the road,
Of life that is left to be,
Our thoughts will often turn to them,
Who sleep 'neath the olive-tree.
From a prison camp publication, May 1942 [21]

Around 17,000 Allied servicemen were evacuated from Crete during the twelve-day battle, mainly from the New Zealand, Australian and British forces; 12,000 men from these forces were left behind to become prisoners of war. Although more than half of the 10,000 Greek soldiers who fought in the conflict were taken prisoner, many of the remaining Greeks chose to disappear into the local population.

From the British, Australian and New Zealand forces more than 1,700 men were killed or died of wounds and a similar number were wounded. More than 330 Greek soldiers were verified as killed and a large number were wounded, but there are no figures for the numbers of Cretans killed or wounded during the battle.

Of the 7,702 New Zealand soldiers on Crete, nearly half were killed, wounded or captured: 671 were killed or died of wounds, 967 were wounded and evacuated, while 2,180 became prisoners of war (of whom more than 20 per cent were wounded). More New Zealanders were killed or wounded than in either the British or Australian armies. This was a significant casualty rate for a country with a population of only 1.6 million.

A relatively high proportion of Australians were taken prisoner (over 3,100 soldiers), because of the failure to evacuate their fighting men at Retimo and on the last night at Sfakia.

The Royal Navy suffered very high casualties in the operations around Crete. Nearly 2,000 sailors were killed, a greater figure than the combined total for the British, Australian and New Zealand forces on Crete. A further 500 were wounded.

Many Germans were also killed and wounded, especially among the airborne forces on the first day of the invasion. Up to 4,000 Germans lost their lives during the entire battle and more than 2,600 were wounded. Of them, around 600 were killed in the air force or in operations at sea.[22]

Left: New Zealand graves at the Commonwealth War Graves Commission cemetery at Suda Bay.

[David Filer]

CASUALTIES

1941

JUNE Axis occupation of Crete

Libyan campaign

1942

JUNE Inglis commands New Zealand Division

1943

NOVEMBER Battle of Leros
1944

AUGUST Death of Hargest
Inglis returns to New Zealand
OCTOBER Germans withdraw to Canea

1945

MAY German surrender on Crete

SEPTEMBER New Zealanders return to Crete

1946

MAY War crimes trial of Student
JUNE Freyberg becomes governor-general
of New Zealand

10

RETRIBUTION AND RECRIMINATION

From the days of the Franco-Prussian war of 1870–71 the German forces had shown an abhorrence for civilians serving as irregular soldiers. They regarded these guerrilla fighters as devious, underhand killers and executed any they captured and, as well, carried out violent reprisals against nearby settlements. This brutal response to people who were often only protecting their homes and families continued during the First World War.

The same attitude was later adopted by Germany's airborne forces. The 'Ten Commandments of the Parachutist', which was sown to the inside of each man's pack, included: 'Against an open foe fight with chivalry, but to a guerrilla extend no quarter.'[1] During and after the battle of Crete, the paratroopers would put this policy into terrible practice.

The paratroopers' prejudices were exacerbated by a number of unfortunate factors on Crete. They had been told that they would be welcomed by the local populace, only to find that Cretan men (and some women and children) fought back with whatever was at hand — guns, knives, axes and even sometimes with rocks. The Cretans killed many of the invaders and then took their weapons and equipment. When the Germans finally advanced they found the bodies of their fallen comrades, often stripped of clothes and boots, swollen and split in the heat, and pecked or chewed by birds and animals. It looked as if the bodies had been deliberately mutilated, although that had occurred in only a small number of cases.

Previous page: Cretan civilian prisoners are forced to assist German paratroopers.

[ATL: Detail of DA-14771]

Right: A wall on the Kondomari memorial showing photographs of the massacre of men from the village.

[David Filer]

Soon, however, stories spread among the Germans that the Cretans had routinely tortured and killed wounded paratroopers and that bodies had been mutilated en masse. The word got back to Goering who told Student to investigate and carry out reprisals. Even before the Allies surrendered, Student issued orders for 'punitive expeditions which must be carried through with exemplary terror', with reprisals including shooting civilians, burning villages and 'extermination of the male population of the territory in question'.[2]

The shootings and burnings began immediately. On 2 June 1941 at Kondomari, east of Maleme, where the 21st Battalion had been based, the members of a paratroop battalion took 60 local men into the olive groves and killed them. The next day they went south to the village of Kandanos, executed 180 civilians, slaughtered the livestock, and torched all the buildings. Meanwhile, at the western port of Kastelli Kisamou where the paratroops had been wiped out early in the battle, 200 Cretan men had been shot after the invaders finally overcame their opponents.

In early August the Germans sent another murderous expedition to villages south of Canea, killing 145 men and two women, and a month later a similar number of Cretans and some men from the British forces were executed in the White Mountains.

Below: German officers visit a Cretan monastery (where the monks secretly assisted Allied escapees).

[E. Neville]

If the Germans expected to subdue the Cretans by these war crimes and other violence, they were disappointed. With their long history of occupation and rebellion, the Cretans knew that brave resistance would always lead to bloody reprisal. They gave no quarter to their enemies and expected none in return, and from the moment the battle was over they began a terrible guerrilla war with the occupiers. One woman from Heraklion recorded the dreadful impact on her family:

> In March 1942 my father was captured . . . They had been betrayed by one of the locals and my father was identified as an accomplice to one of the resistance fighters. On the 3rd of June of that same year he was shot along with eleven others at Heraklion. On the 14th they shot another fifty men . . . Among the fifty who died were my father's brother (a 70 year old priest), his son and his son-in-law.[3]

Despite the fearsome risks, Cretans continued to provide food and shelter to the hundreds of Allied servicemen on the run. These men had either refused to surrender at the end of the battle or had later escaped from the makeshift prison

Right: Tom Moir
*(second from left), an
English soldier and two
Cretans on the island in
May 1943.*
[ATL: DA-12587]

camps set up in the north of the island. It was easy for them to slip under the wire
and head for the hills. If they were captured again they could expect to be returned
to prison, but the Cretans who had looked after them would probably face a firing
squad, as a British serviceman who hid with a family in Canea recalled:

> They welcomed us as their sons, and here I began to learn the hospitality and
> the courage of the Cretan people. They showed us how to escape if the Germans
> should come to the house, knowing full well that they should not escape
> themselves, and that they and their family would certainly be shot . . . We could
> move freely knowing that the whole population was in support of us.[4]

Some of the Allied servicemen joined the Cretan guerrilla bands in the hills and took
part in the dangerous operations against the common enemy. Two of them, Kiwis
Dudley Perkins and Tom Moir, played a significant part in the Cretan resistance.
They were artillerymen who had fought as infantry in the battle, had been taken
prisoner and then escaped from the Galatas prison camp. They moved to the west
coast of the island and eventually made their separate ways back to Egypt, where
they were recruited by military intelligence and returned to Crete in 1943.

  Moir's job was to collect and repatriate the Allied servicemen who were still
roaming free on the island. He arranged for 51 men to be taken off, but then was
captured by a police patrol. He was fortunate to convince the Germans that he had
been on Crete since the battle, and was sent to a prisoner-of-war camp in Germany.
Perkins became the leader of a guerrilla group in the south-west corner of the
White Mountains. His courage and resourcefulness made him famous among the

Cretans, who knew him as 'Kapitan Vasili'. Killed in an ambush in February 1944, Vasili remains a legendary figure in the island's story.

As the years of occupation passed, the terrible round of resistance and reprisals continued. Thousands of Cretans were imprisoned or executed, but gradually the guerrillas, supported by Allied agents, arms and equipment, gained the upper hand. When the wider war turned against Germany in 1944, its High Command reduced the size of the garrison on Crete. With the connivance of the Allies, the remaining German troops were allowed to withdraw from the Heraklion and Retimo regions in October 1944 and to hold only an area around Canea. When the last German commander in Canea surrendered in May 1945, the Cretans had liberated most of their island by themselves, one of few resistance groups in Europe to achieve such a defining feat.

Just over four years earlier the Allied commanders in the battle of Crete had returned to Cairo in a fragile state. Bernard Freyberg came back not only as a defeated general, but to a personal tragedy: he learnt that his stepson had been badly wounded fighting Rommel's forces in Libya and was missing, possibly dead. It took two months for the news to come through that he was alive and a prisoner in a hospital near Naples.

Below: Hargest and his staff officers in Egypt in July 1941. [ATL: DA-01888]

When Freyberg arrived in Egypt he immediately met Prime Minister Fraser and General Wavell. Freyberg wrote that he had 'a difficult meeting' with Wavell, with both men tired and overwrought. Lady Wavell informed him 'that in earlier battles he [Wavell] could always sleep, but that during the last few nights of the Crete campaign he had walked the floor and was unable to rest'.[5]

Meanwhile, Brigadier Hargest was winging his way back to Egypt in a flying boat. He was anxious about the men left behind on Crete and their lack of supplies. He also had time to weigh up his role in the battle and probably knew that he could be criticised for his handling of the defence of Maleme. Was he enough of a politician to know that the best form of defence was attack, and the more dramatic the action the better? Certainly, straight after landing he raced into Cairo, 'dirty & unshaven with only the clothes I possessed not having been removed for 12 days, I pushed my way to the Embassy

Above: Fraser (in the white hat) talking to Kiwi soldiers in Egypt.

[ATL: DA-01105]

& told Gen Wavell & Admiral Cunningham the truth of many things without once knuckling down. Peter Fraser stood by me God Bless him & instead of being ashamed of my appearance was loyally proud.'[6] The next day Hargest met Fraser again and complained not only about Freyberg's leadership on Crete, but also his handling of the retreat in Greece. In his diary he confidently wrote, 'I told my story. I hope it will bear fruit.'[7]

Hargest was not the only one of Freyberg's subordinates to stab him in the back. When Freyberg was asked to send a senior officer to Britain to report on the battle of Crete, he chose Inglis, presuming that he would give a fair account of the operation. Churchill asked to talk to Inglis after he arrived and on 13 June the brigadier went to 10 Downing Street. Unfortunately, it seems that meeting the great man went to his head, as Churchill's minute to his defence chiefs the following day suggests. The prime minister wrote:

> Brigadier Inglis, with whom I had a long talk last night, gave a shocking account of the state of the troops in Crete before the battle . . . I cannot feel that there was any real grip shown by Middle East HQ upon this operation of the defence of Crete. They regarded it as a tiresome commitment, while at the same time acquiescing in its strategic importance . . . I am far from reassured about the tactical conduct of the defence by General Freyberg . . . The whole seems to have been a static defence of positions, instead of the rapid extirpation at all costs of the airborne landing party.[8]

It is clear that Inglis not only commented adversely on Freyberg's defence plan but also criticised the strategic direction of Middle East Command. The details of Churchill's minute also indicate that the brigadier made exaggerated statements about the lack of equipment and the quality of the fighting units. It further appears that he said, incorrectly, that there was no attempt to form a mobile reserve and, without knowing the reason, criticised Freyberg for not obstructing Maleme airfield.

There is no doubt that subordinates should be willing to speak up if the actions of an incompetent commander have led to disaster. In the case of Inglis and Hargest, however, the criticisms they directed towards their general were largely inaccurate and without justification. In fact, their own actions were more open to a critical appraisal.

Nevertheless, it seems that Inglis' comments not only undermined Churchill's enthusiasm for Freyberg but were also a final nail in Wavell's coffin (along with the failure of a concurrent offensive against Rommel's forces in North Africa). When the prime minister's disquiet filtered down to Wavell, he also blamed Freyberg and there was a bitter argument between the two generals. At this time, neither realised that Inglis was the fly in the ointment. Two days after their dispute (which was later resolved), Churchill told Wavell that he was relieved of his command and was to go to India to be the commander-in-chief there. This able and intelligent man, who had been pulled in so many directions with so few resources, understandably felt let down; soon, however, he would be facing a new aggressor in the Far East.

Back in London Churchill demanded a detailed inquiry into the defence of Crete and in late-June an inter-services committee on the campaign began hearing evidence in Cairo. Its members were relatively junior British officers from the three services, with the chairman, Brigadier Guy Salisbury-Jones, having served in Greece and Crete. They were, however, willing to speak their minds, particularly about the support the forces on Crete received from the military staff in Cairo and from the RAF. As Salisbury-Jones later said, 'it was not easy because we naturally were expected to criticise and automatically any criticism we made was indirectly a criticism of General Wavell'.[9]

Freyberg, Puttick, Hargest and other New Zealand officers gave evidence to the committee. Hargest's diary entry shows his own satisfaction with his performance:

> Up & to the Middle East HQ to give evidence before Crete commission. Col Andrew came with me & we gave good evidence. I produced an enlargement of the area — my orders written two days before the attack & my War Diary giving moment to moment happenings — quite a fair type & they were pleased generally.[10]

Unfortunately, the committee, while finding fault with Middle East Command, accepted uncritically the accounts of the officers on the ground. Nor did it analyse in depth the tactics of the defenders. Instead its findings emphasised 'the overwhelming superiority of the German Air Force' and stated that 'the major

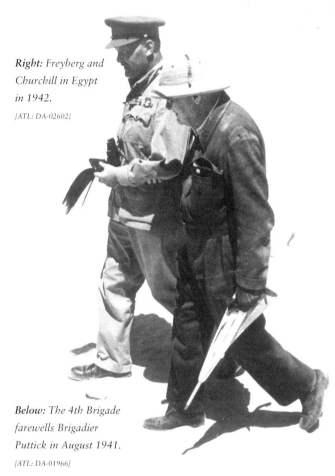

Right: Freyberg and Churchill in Egypt in 1942.

[ATL: DA-02602]

Below: The 4th Brigade farewells Brigadier Puttick in August 1941.

[ATL: DA-01966]

lesson of this campaign was that to defend with a relatively small force an island as large as Crete, lying under the permanent domination of enemy fighter aircraft and out of range of our own, was impossible'.[11]

The committee's report was sent to England early in July 1941. There it was quietly suppressed, ostensibly because it may have betrayed the existence of Ultra (despite the members knowing nothing about the secret intelligence). However, the embarrassment caused to senior officers by the criticism of Middle East Command no doubt also played a part.

Peter Fraser, meanwhile, was trying to resolve the doubts that had been raised about Freyberg's performance on Greece and Crete. He met the general on 7 June to discuss his communications with the New Zealand government, in particular the confused signals about the feasibility of the operation in Greece. Freyberg pointed out the difficulties that the commander of a dominion's forces faced in working inside a larger British structure. Fraser, however, was adamant that Freyberg's first duty was to New Zealand, making it plain that 'in any future case where he doubts the propriety of a proposal he is to give the War Cabinet in Wellington full opportunity of considering the proposal, with his views on it'.[12] From then on, over the next four years, Freyberg kept Fraser well informed about Allied plans and, when necessary, as commander of 2NZEF, used the powers of his charter to advance New Zealand's position.

The prime minister also had a stern discussion with his general about the complaint (largely from Hargest) that he did not discuss his plans enough with senior officers. According to Fraser, Freyberg took his comments 'in excellent spirit' and 'proposed at a very early date to confer with his senior officers with a view to removing any misunderstanding'.[13] The outcome of this was

Above: *New Zealand troops link up with the defenders of Tobruk during the Libyan campaign in late-1941.*

[ATL: DA-01668]

that Hargest would write to Fraser some months later saying that he was now very happy with the way Freyberg ran his conferences.

In contrast, Hargest's criticisms of Freyberg's actions on Greece were not supported in a separate report on the campaign; in fact, the general 'happily described it as an unsolicited testimonial'.[14] However, Fraser was still not convinced that he was the right man to lead 2NZEF through the battles yet to come. The old Scot showed his canniness by consulting the Chief of the Imperial General Staff, General Dill, while in London in August 1941. Dill sought the opinions of General Wavell in India and General Auchinleck in Egypt, and both sent largely positive replies, stating how Freyberg's training and efficiency had produced a high-quality division, and while noting his problems with subordinates, they said it would be a mistake to remove him from the command of the New Zealand Division. Even then Fraser was not totally reassured and it was not until after the Libyan campaign at the end of 1941 that he seemed fully reconciled to Freyberg remaining in command.

However, it took longer for the general to return to Churchill's favour. As Paul Freyberg has written, his father 'was consigned to the prime ministerial doghouse, and for twelve months there was no communication between them'.[15] But Freyberg was more upset that no message of support had been sent to the troops who had fought so doggedly than about receiving condolences himself. Eventually, after he was wounded in North Africa in mid-1942, Churchill sent him an affectionate telegram and their old friendship was re-established. Even so, Freyberg would later jokingly say, 'I have taken part in all of Winston's disasters', by which he meant Antwerp in 1914, Gallipoli in 1915 and Greece and Crete in 1941.[16]

The general's main concern after his return from Crete was not to deal with all the enquiries and recriminations, but to rebuild his battered force. One-third of the manpower of the New Zealand Division had been lost in Greece and Crete, along with most of their equipment. Reinforcements had to be integrated into the units back in Egypt, while weapons and vehicles had to be replaced and training reinstated. Yet the morale among the men who had gone through the campaigns was generally high. Even the survivors of the 22nd Battalion were unbowed, according to Lieutenant Colonel Andrew:

> We know now that we can deal with the enemy even with his tanks and/or aeroplanes, that he does not like night work or the bayonet, and that on the ground he is no match for our men. Even though we had to withdraw for eleven days we had our 'tails up' in defeat.[17]

Freyberg knew that not all his subordinate commanders had performed well in Greece and Crete, although it appears that he did not fully understand why Maleme had been lost. In any event, his behaviour towards his subordinates was very different from the way some had behaved towards him. There was no witch-hunt and he took full responsibility for the defeat. However, a number of officers (including Puttick and Macky) were sent back to New Zealand, where they busied themselves organising reinforcements for 2NZEF and preparing to defend the country against Japanese aggression. There were rumours in the 22nd Battalion

Below: A New Zealand anti-tank gun in action in Libya. [ATL: DA-10744]

that Lieutenant Colonel Andrew was going home, but he was still in charge when the Libyan campaign began in November 1941, while Hargest also remained in command of the 5th Brigade.

The central aim of the Libyan campaign was for the 8th Army to defeat Rommel's forces and his Italian allies in eastern Libya and relieve the troops besieged in Tobruk. The New Zealand Division played a key role, with the 4th and 6th brigades opening the corridor to Tobruk, while the 5th Brigade covered the enemy-occupied port of Bardia and the coast road. Unfortunately, Hargest had to spread his forces across a wide area, with two battalions some 20 kilometres south of brigade headquarters and the 22nd Battalion fifteen kilometres to the north. On the morning of 27 November a massive force of German tanks rolled into the command area and, despite a brave fight, Hargest and most of his men were forced to surrender.

On an escarpment away to the north, Andrew and the 22nd Battalion realised that their headquarters had been overrun. Soon, however, they were engaged by German forces moving along the coast road, with fighting continuing throughout the day until the enemy withdrew. By now Andrew was short of food and ammunition and out of radio contact with other units. As a New Zealand writer later suggested, the colonel 'began to realise that history was repeating itself: his battalion was again isolated as it had been at Maleme'.[18]

Andrew then took a similar decision to that made on Crete six months before: he abandoned his defences without consulting his superiors and moved his force south until he was in contact with other New Zealand units. This time, fortunately, no disaster ensued. In fact, with Hargest gone, Andrew was given the temporary command of the 5th Brigade, before going back to his own battalion in early December. He took part in the pursuit of the Axis forces as they pulled back from Tobruk, before the entire New Zealand Division returned to Egypt.

Andrew's abandonment of his position on the escarpment did not go unnoticed at the highest levels of the 8th Army. However, he was already earmarked to return to New Zealand and on 3 February 1942 said goodbye to his beloved battalion. Despite his old-fashioned approach to discipline, he retained the respect and admiration of his men long after he had gone. Back home, he also played his part in readying the country for a Japanese attack.

Hargest, meanwhile, had been taken to Italy as a prisoner of war and had been placed in a special camp for senior Allied officers at an old fortress in the hills outside Florence. Along with another New Zealand brigadier and four other officers, he made one of the famous escapes of the war, tunnelling out of the castle in March 1943. After many adventures the two Kiwi brigadiers reached neutral Switzerland, and then separately made the dangerous crossing through occupied France to Spain. Hargest eventually was taken via Gibraltar to England where he wrote an account of the escape (called *Farewell Campo 12*) which became a runaway best-seller. He also created a new military role for himself, as New Zealand's observer with the D-Day armies, but his adventures were cut short when he was killed by a shell burst in Normandy in August 1944.

Above: Hargest in the disguise he wore while crossing southern France. [ATL: DA-11320]

Above: Inglis in Egypt in August 1942. [ATL: DA-02567]

By this stage of the war the New Zealand Division had fought across North Africa and up through Italy, playing a significant role in the gradual defeat of the Axis forces. Freyberg was not always in charge of the division: at times he held more senior positions, or was away in Britain or New Zealand, or was wounded or injured. In June 1942 he was badly wounded in North Africa and Brigadier Inglis took up the role he had no doubt been aspiring to, the temporary command of the division. He had the misfortune, however, to lead the New Zealanders through two terrible battles the following month in which a lack of British armoured support resulted in 2,500 Kiwi casualties. Mentally and physically exhausted, he went back to Cairo in early August.

Inglis later took the lead in developing New Zealand's own armoured brigade and commanded it in Italy in mid-1944. But by now he was drinking more heavily and this may have played a part in Freyberg overlooking him whenever a temporary divisional commander was needed. The general clearly preferred up-and-coming men like Kippenberger. Eventually, Inglis wrote an insulting letter to Freyberg, asked to be relieved of his post and went back to New Zealand. He found a new lease of life, however, immediately the war in Europe was over, taking up senior legal positions with the military government in the British zone in occupied Germany.

Freyberg stayed in command of the division till the end of the war and beyond, when he was appointed governor-general of New Zealand. His son has recorded that it was 'the longest period of continuous and unbroken service by a senior officer in an operational command in any of the three services of the British and Commonwealth forces during the Second World War'.[19] He finished his military life heaped with honours and accolades, but one part of his career, the conflict on Crete, always seemed to undermine his other achievements. Crete had been his

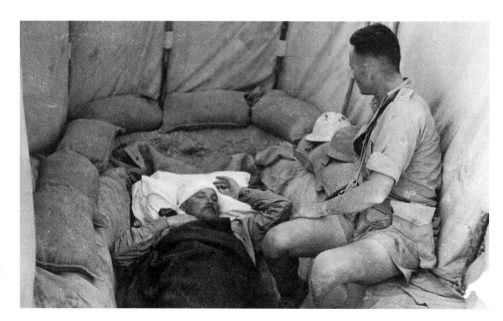

Right: Freyberg lies in a slit trench, after being wounded in mid-1942.

[ATL: DA-02558]

RETURN TO CRETE

Just after the end of the Second World War, while the New Zealand Division remained in Italy, General Freyberg organised a return visit to Crete for the veterans of the conflict. He wanted to thank the Cretans for their brave assistance during and after the battle and honour the New Zealand dead.

There were around 100 veterans still with the division in Italy and another 40 came from Egypt and Britain. They were accompanied by a guard of honour from the Maori Battalion and the band of the 5th Brigade. In late-September the party sailed to Crete on the cruiser *Ajax*, which had carried New Zealanders from Greece to Crete in 1941 and had been bombed and damaged during the later evacuation of the island.

The party landed on 29 September 1945 and over the next three days visited Canea, Galatas and Maleme. The Kiwis were welcomed everywhere and, as Denis McLean has written, 'All found their short visit deeply moving and marking . . . The people lined the roads, offering flowers and small gifts, and the villagers overwhelmed them with warm hospitality.'[20]

Kippenberger spoke for the entire party when he said to the people of Galatas that the Kiwis had returned:

To pay homage to Cretan valour during the bitter fighting of 1941; to thank them for the risks they had run for our prisoners, free and living in hiding with them during the occupation and to pay our last respects to our own dead. We wished to visit their graves, which had been so well and lovingly tended — clandestinely — under the German regime and then to hand them to the Cretan people for all time.[21]

The following day 15,000 Cretans came to a memorial service at the Commonwealth cemetery at Suda Bay. Wreaths were laid on the graves and the central cross, and a Maori choir sang as the chaplains conducted the service. Freyberg spoke of the battle and the men who had died, saying that 'the fight to hold Crete was the hardest and most savage campaign of the New Zealand Division'. He then read a special message from Peter Fraser, stating the country's gratitude to the people of Greece and Crete:

We shall never forget all of you personally and what those associated with you have done for our men during the whole of this war . . . We realise that you have clothed and fed our men when you were in want yourselves and that in doing so you suffered hardship and ran great personal risk. I send sincerest wishes for the happiness and prosperity of your country from your friends and comrades in New Zealand.[22]

These were not empty words. In the immediate post-war years the Greek (and Cretan) economy faced hard times and much of New Zealand's foreign aid (both official and private) was directed towards assisting the people of Greece.

Above left: Lunch at Galatas for the returning Kiwis.
[ATL: DA-08448]

Above right: The Maori choir during the memorial service at Suda Bay.
[ATL: DA-08460]

battle, he had held the full command, there had been a chance of winning it, and yet he had been defeated. He remained obsessed with the battle until the end of his days, as his chief administrative officer noted:

> The General himself talked about Crete so often, and sometimes seemed to drag it into the conversation. I cannot remember him reviving any of the other battles in the same way — not Greece or any in North Africa. To those who listened it sounded as if he was on the defensive, and in his heart thought that perhaps he should have acted in some other way; but whether or not that is the case, there is no doubt that the campaign was on his mind above all others.[23]

General Student had returned to Germany in June 1941 a troubled man. He may have won the battle of Crete, but his units had suffered many casualties, the highest proportion in any German engagement in the war up to that time. Worst of all, his brainchild, the airborne division, had been virtually annihilated.

When he and other senior officers went to Hitler's headquarters to meet the Führer, he hoped to make the case for rebuilding and expanding the airborne forces. But Hitler had come to another conclusion, as he told Student after lunch:

Below: Graves of paratroopers killed on Crete. [Filer collection]

> Of course, you know, General, we shall never do another airborne operation. Crete proved that the days of parachute troops are over. The parachute arm is one that relies entirely on surprise. In the meantime the surprise factor has exhausted itself.[24]

As Student later said: 'Crete was the grave of the German parachutist.'[25] From this point on they were mainly used as elite infantry on both the eastern and western fronts. The New Zealand Division encountered them again in Italy, at Cassino, where they proved tough and resourceful opponents, and in the battles further north. One group of Kiwis, however, did see German paratroopers descend once more into battle from the skies, on the Aegean island of Leros late in 1943.

When Italy surrendered in September 1943, Churchill decided to take control of the Dodecanese Islands which had previously been under Italian occupation. The small British force sent to the islands included

Above: A dead paratrooper after a New Zealand attack in northern Italy.
[ATL: DA-08369]

around 100 New Zealanders serving in the Long Range Desert Group. The Germans reacted with a powerful counter-attack from the sea and the air, and on 12 November the Kiwis saw hundreds of paratroopers jumping from Junker 52s above the island. They were soon engaged by the Allies, but the overall assault was too strong and once again the Luftwaffe dominated the skies. When the British commander surrendered Leros a few days later, most of the Kiwis had to make their own escape from the island.

It was like Crete all over again, but on a smaller scale. Churchill had pushed ahead with an adventure with minimal forces and not enough air cover, and the soldiers on the ground had suffered the consequences.

Churchill, however, had ordered a build-up of British airborne forces after the battle of Crete, and the Americans took similar steps. Allied paratroop units were dropped, with varying success, in Sicily and Italy and later over France, the Netherlands and Germany. Ironically, Student was a commander of German forces at Arnhem in September 1944 where a massive Allied airborne assault was defeated.

After the war Student was imprisoned by the British and investigated for war crimes. But he was not charged with ordering the reprisals which led to the massacre of hundreds of civilians on Crete (and a later Greek request that he be extradited to face trial in Athens was declined). Instead the British charged him with war crimes relating to the mistreatment and murder of prisoners of war by German forces on Crete. Among the witnesses in his favour were two opponents on the Crete battlefield, Baron von der Heydte and Lindsay Inglis. Although Student was found guilty on three charges, his responsibility remained in doubt; the finding and sentence were not confirmed and he was soon released from prison on medical grounds.[26]

He would live on for another 30 years, before dying in 1978 (fifteen years after Bernard Freyberg) at the ripe old age of 88.

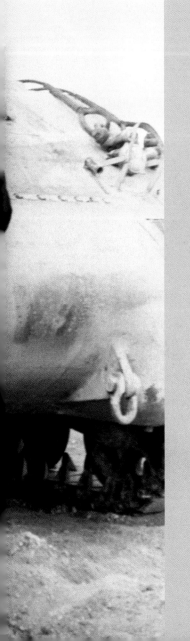

11

A RECKONING

The battle of Crete was controversial from the moment the troops departed, and has remained so ever since. As the fighting neared its end and in the weeks following, it became the accepted truth among the Allies that they had been beaten by a dominant and unopposed Luftwaffe, which had simply bombed and strafed them off the island.

On 24 May 1941 Freyberg had signalled Wavell that the scale of the air attack had been 'savage' and that 'with the lack of any air support whatsoever the result with tired troops must always be in the balance'; two days later he added that 'a small, ill-equipped and immobile force such as ours cannot stand up against the concentrated bombing that we have been faced with during the last seven days'.[1]

Peter Fraser endorsed these statements in his report to the New Zealand government in early June:

> It seems clear to me now that with the means at Freyberg's disposal the island was in fact indefensible against the scale of attack which actually developed. It seems to me also, that it should have been as clear before the decision to defend Crete as it is now, that troops without adequate air protection (which it was known could not be provided) would be in a hopeless position, though obviously the scale of German air attack was larger and more intense than was foreseen.[2]

A few weeks later the inter-services committee investigating the campaign went even further, stating that German control of the air had made it 'impossible' to defend Crete. Variations on these themes have been repeated over the years, both by veterans and historians up to the present day.[3]

However, from early on there were dissenting views, particularly from one of the heroes of the battle, Howard Kippenberger. After the war he was appointed Editor-in-Chief of the New Zealand official war histories and quickly recruited Dan Davin

Previous page:
Brigadier Inglis with the
New Zealand Defence
Minister, Frederick
Jones, in Egypt in 1943.
[ATL: DA-02985]

Right: Kippenberger
speaking at the 2NZEF
unit histories conference
in July 1946. [ATL: PAColl-
0783-2-0339]

Left: Victoria Cross
winners from two world
wars on the steps of
Parliament in 1945,
including Andrew (back
left), Hinton (front left),
Upham (front centre)
and Hulme (front,
second from right).

[ATL: 1/2-031707]

(then at Oxford University Press) to write the volume on Crete. Kippenberger wrote
to Davin that he had been 'bitterly disappointed during the battle, bitterly angry
afterwards. Some of that feeling remains but it must not appear in your volume.'[4]

Kip's disappointment and anger was not because of the lack of air support; rather
he believed that many of the New Zealand commanders had failed on Crete, and
that their actions (or inaction) had been the margin between victory and defeat.
However, he knew that, with most of them still alive, it would be unacceptable
to openly castigate them in an official history. He reserved his opinions to private
communications, writing to one senior officer about 'the story of Maleme and
commanders 5 Brigade and 22 Battalion working out very badly indeed. Hargest's
flabbiness and lack of grip dreadfully evident. Puttick not much better. Inglis all
talk . . . and nothing done.'[5] In comments on Davin's draft he remarked:

> I have many things for which to be grateful to Puttick, much friendship
> with Hargest and Andrew . . . The failure in each case seems to me to have
> been that they answered all questions pessimistically, that they saw all
> dangers, real, imagined or possible, that none made any effort to dictate or
> control events, that they were utterly without any offensive spirit, and that
> invariably in each case, they adopted the course that made victory impossible
> and defeat inevitable. Not the minor mistakes all commanders make . . . but
> fundamental mistakes, irretrievable by the valour and devotion of those under
> their command.[6]

Above: Puttick and Hargest. [ATL: DA-14418]

Davin was writing an official history and had to pull his (and Kip's) punches. He did, however, produce a comprehensive account of the Crete campaign and raised a number of questions about the decisions made by various commanders which later writers would follow up in a more critical way. The actions of the three New Zealand brigadiers — Hargest, Puttick and Inglis — and the battalion commanders of the 5th Brigade — in particular, Andrew — would all eventually be called into question.

It is fair to say that Andrew's greatest failure was, after the stress and strain of a day of intense fighting, to lose sight of the importance of retaining Point 107. It was the key position in preventing the Germans from using Maleme airfield and, although he knew this, he still withdrew the companies holding the hill.

Sixty years later historian Chris Pugsley suggested that Andrew had 'lost his nerve', a statement that drew a heated response from some of the remaining men who had been on Point 107. One of them replied that the colonel was 'one of New Zealand's bravest soldiers' and that he 'did not panic; he made a reasoned decision on the situation as he believed it to be on the evidence he had available'.[7] Certainly, Andrew was unlucky: lack of communications had led him to conclude that half the battalion had been overrun, his tank attack had literally broken down and his brigadier had failed to order a wider counter-attack. However, reinforcements were on the way and he could have held on. If any crisis on Crete called for the terrible decision to fight to the last round and the last man, it was keeping Point 107 in Allied hands. As Kippenberger later noted (in a criticism of Andrew, not his men), 'this was the case where it was the duty of an infantry battalion to fight to the finish'.[8]

Andrew was not the only officer in the 5th Brigade to be censured later. The commanders of the 21st and 23rd battalions (Allen and Leckie) were also criticised for not counter-attacking off their own bat on 20 May. They had, however, no reason to believe that the 22nd Battalion was in trouble; in fact, Hargest had been reassuring, and they were surprised to find a defeated Andrew arriving with his men in their lines at the end of first day of battle.

It is Hargest who has to take much of the blame for the loss of Maleme and, as a result, for the Allies' defeat on Crete. Like commanders in the previous world war, he had placed his headquarters many kilometres behind the key defence positions and, when communications broke down, he was soon out of touch with his subordinates. Three specific strikes can be made against his decision-making during the battle: he failed to order the planned counter-attack by the 23rd Battalion even after Andrew requested it; instead of clearly telling Andrew to stay on Point 107 and wait for reinforcements, he gave him the option of leaving; and he did not bolster the counter-attack on the second night of the battle by including the men of the 23rd. He was also overly negative about using his men in the proposed counter-attack the following night.

In fact, Hargest appeared confused and exhausted until well after Maleme was lost. It seems likely that he was affected by a recurrence of shell shock and, considering this known condition, should not have been in command at all. It was only because of Hargest's ambition and the intervention of Peter Fraser on behalf of a parliamentary colleague that he was at the front. This political interference in a military appointment had a disastrous result and Fraser, therefore, has to take some responsibility for the debacle on Crete as well.

Another New Zealand brigadier who dithered on the first day of battle was Puttick. As Kippenberger wrote, to 'destroy the scattered forces in the Prison Valley' Freyberg had given Puttick 'the necessary troops, at the very least expecting them to be used'.[9] But for most of the day Puttick prevaricated and when he finally counter-attacked into the valley it was too late to be successful. He later commented that he considered that the 'only virtues' of the counter-attack were to 'assist morale and impose caution on the enemy'.[10]

It seems likely that, despite intensive training, some of the senior officers in the New Zealand Division at the time of Crete had yet to come to grips with modern tactics and were still fighting the battles of the First World War. As British historian Alan Clark wrote 20 years later:

Above: Freyberg and Kippenberger (Egypt, 1942). [Sir John White]

> . . . the qualities of the senior officers of the New Zealand Division (with the exception of Inglis and Kippenberger) were not suited to the new methods of warfare, and an inadequate complement to the bravery of the men, and the tactical skill and resourcefulness of the junior officers and N.C.O's. Men like Hargest, Puttick, Andrew were brave . . . they were calm and they were experienced. But this was 1941. The War was hardly a year old; 'experience' still referred to the battles, the drawn-out linear deadlock of 1914-18, when flanks were all-important, when the rear was always secure, when the reserves should never be used in the opening hours.[11]

Inglis and Kippenberger, however, were not the only exceptions, as the Australian commanders at Retimo and the British at Heraklion successfully carried out Freyberg's plan of holding the key positions and immediately counter-attacking any footholds the Germans gained. This is one battle where British commanders on the ground in the main performed better than many of their New Zealander equivalents. And Inglis, too, would face his own crisis of conscience later in the battle when he failed to take up the leadership of the Force Reserve, thereby helping ensure its destruction. His fierce critic Ian Stewart, in his 1966 account of

Above: Damaged German planes litter the airfield at Maleme.

[ATL: DA-02059]

the conflict, concluded that: 'the truth must be that Inglis had based his actions throughout . . . not upon provisional acceptance of an order already twice confirmed, but upon the ill-placed and mistaken conjecture that it would be rescinded.'[12]

General Freyberg's actions on Crete were also criticised by Clark and Stewart, but it was not until after the Ultra secret was revealed in the 1970s that the knives truly came out. Despite Paul Freyberg's attempt to defend his father, it was widely assumed that any commander with the level of knowledge about the enemy's plans that he had, should have been able to win the battle. In 1987 Antony Beevor added the damning criticism that Freyberg misunderstood the German strategy and, by emphasising the threat of a sea invasion at the expense of the aerial assault, caused the Allies' defeat.

In fact, Freyberg did see the airborne invasion as the primary threat and planned accordingly. But Beevor is correct, however, in that Freyberg misinterpreted Ultra information about the site of the sea invasion and that this led to the counter-attack at Maleme starting several hours late and thus not achieving its objectives. Although there were good reasons for Freyberg's interpretation, the outcome was clearly in the Germans' favour. His failure to launch a further counter-attack the following night and his subsequent attempt to establish a 'secure' defence line east of Maleme suggest that he too, under intense pressure, was reverting to First World War thinking. He may also have been influenced by another concern, as he indicated after the war:

> There was another factor that weighed with me. I had the bulk of the New
> Zealand Division in Crete. If it were lost it would be a crushing blow to
> New Zealand. This was the second time within a month that the whole of
> the New Zealand Forces were placed in jeopardy.[13]

There can be no question that Churchill and Wavell had given Freyberg an
extremely difficult task on Crete. He faced equipment and air-defence shortages,
and the RAF had prevented the obstruction of the airfields. Furthermore, he did
not have enough men to cover many of the possible landing sites for the German
airborne forces. In addition to the undefended land to the west of the Tavronitis
River, there were large gaps between Platanias and Galatas and to the south of
all the defended areas. Freyberg was lucky in that his opponent, General Student,
made the terrible mistake of dropping most of his force in a scatter-gun approach
right over the defences, but unlucky in that there were still enough surviving
paratroopers to pressure the Kiwi commanders into withdrawing from Maleme.

Freyberg has been criticised for not going to the Maleme front himself but he
was in command of the entire battle occurring across a 140-kilometre span of
the island. He could not abandon his Canea headquarters to focus on one sector
alone and had no choice but to rely on his subordinates. In any event, poor
communications meant he was unable to maintain the detailed overview of his
Kiwi commanders that he had employed during the previous year's training. There
can be no doubt that if Freyberg had known within half an hour of Andrew's
decision to withdraw from Point 107, he would have sent an order to hold firm
and then would have told Hargest to launch the planned counter-attack. Because
of the problems with radio and telephone links, however, he did not hear about the
withdrawal until the following morning, by which time it was too late to respond.

After the war General Student acknowledged that if the New Zealanders had
made an organised counter-attack during the first night, they 'would probably have
succeeded in routing the much battered and exhausted remnants of the Assault
Regiment'.[14] If the remaining Germans had been pushed away from the airfield
and Point 107, they would not have been able to send in the reinforcements of the
Mountain Division. Although the Luftwaffe's transport aircraft could land on the
beach or even on roads, there was a high risk they would be damaged and return
take-offs would be very difficult. The Germans on the ground would eventually
have run out of men and supplies and been forced to surrender. It is clear, however,
that even before this, Student's superiors would have told him to cut his losses and
abandon the operation.

In the end, the battle of Crete was won by the Germans because they seized
Maleme airfield; it was lost by the Allies because they gave up Point 107 and over
the following nights failed to put in a successful counter-attack to retake the lost
ground. The determination of the German commanders granted them victory; the
inertia of some of their Kiwi counterparts gave them defeat.

Responsibility for success or failure lies with the commanders, not their men, who on both sides fought with courage and skill. The Kiwis took part in more close-quarter, hand-to-hand combat in this campaign than in any other during the war. They came out of the battle feeling that they were more than a match for an elite German force, the paratroopers, who had suffered so many casualties that they were never again used in a large-scale airborne assault.

Thousands of men, invaders and defenders, were killed and wounded during the struggle for Crete and many more Allied servicemen disappeared into prison camps for the duration. Yet this dreadful sacrifice seems to have had little strategic purpose. Immediately the battle was over, Crete became one of the backwaters of the war, for both the Allies and the Axis. Hitler, who promptly switched his interest to Operation Barbarossa (the attack on the Soviet Union), said he did 'not intend to make Crete into a German strong-point',[15] and the Germans never turned Suda Bay into a major naval base, nor did they use the airfields to launch a bombing campaign against the British in North Africa. They seemed content to simply have denied the island to the Allies.

The arguments the Allies had made for defending Crete were not strategically important. The primary reason that the battle occurred at all appears to be Churchill's desire to give the Germans a 'bloody nose' following the humiliation in Greece. It is clear now that if the Allies had won the conflict, Crete would soon have been a noose around their necks. To deter a further German assault a garrison of at least a division in size would have been needed, which would have been better employed fighting Rommel in North Africa. To oppose Luftwaffe bombing raids, proper support from RAF fighters would also have been required and this, too, could have been more usefully deployed elsewhere. The army and air force would have needed constant supply via the sea across the well-bombed routes of the eastern Mediterranean and into the equally vulnerable port of Suda Bay. In fact, the commanders of the Royal Navy and the RAF in the Mediterranean were privately grateful that Crete had been lost, as they told Freyberg just after the war ended.[16]

Charles Upham, who became famous because of his actions on Crete, later said that 'the Germans made no use of Crete whatsoever in the war and we wouldn't have made any use of it . . . it wasn't a great loss to the British except in morale and that sort of thing. The Allies were sick of getting beaten all the time, that was really the biggest loss of Crete.'[17] Historian Peter Calvocoressi, who had spent the war working on Ultra intelligence, went further, writing:

> The battle of Crete was one of those operations which appear in retrospect tragically futile. Crete was not prepared for defence and should not have been defended. Its loss was without strategic significance. So was its capture . . . People died: that is all. The very pointlessness of it makes Crete one of the purest arguments against war.[18]

Yet, despite the defeat, there were some positives for the Allies. Germany's airborne division had been shattered and Student's dream of using it, and larger forces, in further invasions from the sky would not be realised. A significant number of German troops were soon tied up occupying the island's towns and ports and in costly anti-guerrilla operations in the mountains.

After the war some veterans and historians began to claim a greater significance for the entire Greek campaign, and for Crete as its final act. The argument was made that because Hitler had postponed his invasion of the Soviet Union in order to conquer Yugoslavia and Greece, his forces had not been able to take Moscow or Leningrad before the Russian winter set in and halted their advance. The bow was drawn even longer to suggest that this in turn led to Nazi Germany's failure on the eastern front and its ultimate defeat.

Other historians countered that Operation Barbarossa would have been delayed anyway, citing a late spring thaw in eastern Europe, slow preparation of airfields, and a tardy distribution of trucks and oil to the German forces. If Crete itself had an impact on the fighting in the Soviet Union, it was most likely because of the loss of so many transport planes during the battle, with 150 completely destroyed and 165 heavily damaged.[19] As Antony Beevor has written, 'German production of transport aircraft never caught up in time for the Stalingrad airlift' in the winter of 1942–43. He added, however, that 'the notion that the battles of Greece and Crete delayed Barbarossa with fatal effect was nothing more than wishful consolation'.[20]

The conflict in Crete is now remembered by many historians as the first large-scale airborne assault in history, for the early use of Ultra intelligence by the Allies and because the margin between victory and defeat was so close. It has a special interest for New Zealanders because of the decisive role played by our soldiers and commanders.

In the immediate aftermath, however, the battle primarily concerned the men who fought there, the families of the dead and wounded, and the people of Crete. This was the last in a long line of struggles for their island and once again they opposed the invader with desperate courage and willing sacrifice. As the British writer and soldier Patrick Leigh Fermor eloquently stated in Crete on the fortieth anniversary of the battle:

> Ideas change, men die, and, in time, all monuments fall. But perhaps something indestructible will survive; the spirit that guided the inhabitants of this island; something indefinable and noble and inspiring and inspired and as brilliant as the air and light which shines on your mountains.[21]

Above: Two Cretans who fought the Germans during the occupation, one in traditional dress and the other in uniform.

[ATL: Detail of DA-07897]

NOTES AND SOURCES

INTRODUCTION

1. There are many ways to spell Greek place names in English. I have seen the main port in western Crete spelt as Hania, Xania, Khania, Chania and Canea. I have chosen to follow the spellings generally used by the Allies during the war, and by most historians writing in English since then.
2. Updated statistics (March 2010) from the Commonwealth War Graves Commission.
3. Megan Hutching ed., *A Unique Sort of Battle*, HarperCollins, Auckland, 2001; Jill McAra, *Stand for New Zealand*, Wilson Scott, Christchurch, 2004.
4. Julian Thompson, *Dunkirk*, Sidgwick & Jackson, London, 2008, p.217.
5. I am grateful for the assistance of the owner of this film, John Irwin. Other researchers can contact him at: johni@clear.net.nz

CHAPTER 1: PASSAGES TO WAR

1. Denis McLean, *Howard Kippenberger*, Random House, Auckland, 2008, pp.125–126.
2. F.L.W. Wood, *The New Zealand People at War*, War History Branch, Department of Internal Affairs, Wellington, 1958, p.70.
3. Paul Freyberg, *Bernard Freyberg V.C.*, Hodder & Stoughton, London, 1991, p.139.
4. *Documents Relating to New Zealand's Participation in the Second World War 1939–45*, Vol. I, War History Branch, Department of Internal Affairs, Wellington, 1949, p.30.
5. Ibid.
6. Geoffrey Cox, *A Tale of Two Battles*, William Kimber, London, 1987, p.57.
7. John McLeod, *Myth and Reality*, Reed Methuen, Auckland, 1986, p.36.
8. Archives New Zealand, WA II 8, File 0, Freyberg Correspondence, 12 February 1940.
9. Sir John White, Interview for 'Freyberg V.C.' series.
10. Freyberg, op cit, p.219.
11. Charles Bennett, Interview for 'Freyberg V.C.' series.
12. W.G. Stevens, *Freyberg, V.C. The Man*, A.H. & A.W. Reed, Wellington, 1965, p.26.
13. Antony Beevor, *Crete: The Battle and the Resistance*, Penguin, London, 1992, pp.89, 91.
14. Cox, op cit, p.43.

CHAPTER 2: A GREEK TRAGEDY

1. W.G. McClymont, *To Greece*, War History Branch, Department of Internal Affairs, Wellington, 1959, p.89.
2. Martin Gilbert, *Finest Hour*, Heinemann, London, 1983, p.1,010.
3. *Documents Relating to New Zealand's Participation in the Second World War 1939–45*, Vol. I, War History Branch, Department of Internal Affairs, Wellington, 1949, p.207.
4. Ibid, p.243.
5. Ian McGibbon ed., *The Oxford Companion to New Zealand Military History*, Oxford University Press, Auckland, 2000, p.205.
6. Charles Upham, Interview for 'Freyberg V.C.' series.
7. John McLeod, *Myth and Reality*, Reed Methuen, Auckland, 1986, p.31.
8. Laurie Cropp, Interview for 'Freyberg V.C.' series.
9. Paul Freyberg, *Bernard Freyberg V.C.*, Hodder & Stoughton, London, 1991, p.256.
10. McClymont, op cit, p.417.
11. Ibid, pp.417–419.
12. Phil Hanna, Interview for 'Freyberg V.C.' series.
13. Freyberg, op cit, p.244.
14. Tony Simpson, *Operation Mercury*, Hodder & Stoughton, London, 1981, p.21.

CHAPTER 3: BEST-LAID PLANS

1. I.McD.G. Stewart, *The Struggle for Crete*, Oxford University Press, London, 1966, p.44.
2. Angus Ross, *23 Battalion*, War History Branch, Department of Internal Affairs, Wellington, 1959, p.59.
3. Martin Gilbert, *Finest Hour*, Heinemann, London, 1983, p.1,072.
4. Ibid, p.1,077.
5. Paul Freyberg, *Bernard Freyberg V.C.*, Hodder & Stoughton, London, 1991, p.267.
6. Ibid, pp.3–4, 279–289.
7. Research interviews for 'Freyberg V.C.' series.
8. See also W.G. Stevens, *Freyberg, V.C. The Man*, A.H. & A.W. Reed, Wellington, 1965, pp.32, 89.
9. Matthew Wright, *Freyberg's War*, Penguin, Auckland, 2005, p.56.
10. Geoffrey Cox, *A Tale of Two Battles*, William Kimber, London, 1987, p.56.
11. *Documents Relating to New Zealand's Participation in the Second World War 1939–45*, Vol. I, War History Branch, Department of Internal Affairs, Wellington, 1949, p.285.
12. Ibid, pp.286, 291.
13. Freyberg, op cit, p.292.
14. Haddon Donald, Interview for 'Freyberg V.C.' series.
15. Freyberg, op cit, p.273.
16. Wright, op cit, p.59.
17. Cox, op cit, p.110.
18. Antony Beevor, *Crete: The Battle and the Resistance*, Penguin, London, 1992, p.98; Laurie Barber & John Tonkin-Covell, *Freyberg: Churchill's Salamander*, Century Hutchinson, Auckland, 1989, pp.20, 30.
19. D.M. Davin, *Crete*, War History Branch, Department of Internal Affairs, Wellington, 1953, p.48.
20. Stewart, op cit, p.125.
21. Howard Kippenberger, *Infantry Brigadier*, Oxford University Press, London, 1949, p.50.
22. Stewart, op cit, p.120.
23. Dan Davin, Interview for 'Freyberg V.C.' series.
24. Jack Griffith, Interview for 'Freyberg V.C.' series.
25. Archives New Zealand, IA 181/32/2 Part 1, 17 October 1949.
26. Beevor, op cit, p.351.
27. Ibid, p.90.
28. Ibid, p.78.
29. Wright, op cit, p.62.
30. Wikipedia: Fallschirmjager; Lone Sentry: Parachutists, German (WW II U.S. Intelligence Bulletin, September 1942). Accessed December 2009.

31. Barber & Tonkin-Covell, op cit, p.47; Haddon Donald, *In Peace and War*, Fraser Books, Masterton, 2005, p.29.

32. Denis McLean, *Howard Kippenberger*, Random House, Auckland, 2008, p.167.

33. Matthew Wright, *Battle for Crete*, Reed, Auckland, 2003, p.112.

34. Archives New Zealand, DA 52/10/10, Hargest, J. Extracts from Letters and Diary, 8 February 1941 to 25 June 1941.

35. Cox, op cit, p.67.

CHAPTER 4: DAY ONE: CANEA, MALEME AND GALATAS

1. Baron von der Heydte, *Daedalus Returned*, Hutchinson, London, 1958, p.52.

2. Costas Hadjipateras & Maria Fafalios, *Crete 1941 Eyewitnessed*, Efstathiadis Group, Anixi Attikis, 1989, p.78.

3. John McLeod, *Myth and Reality*, Reed Methuen, Auckland, 1986, p.35.

4. Haddon Donald, Interview for 'Freyberg V.C.' series.

5. Antony Beevor, *Crete: The Battle and the Resistance*, Penguin, London, 1992, p.107.

6. Hadjipateras & Fafalios, op cit, p.88.

7. D.M. Davin, *Crete*, War History Branch, Department of Internal Affairs, Wellington, 1953, p.159.

8. Charles Bennett, Interview for 'Freyberg V.C.' series.

9. Jim Henderson, *22 Battalion*, War History Branch, Department of Internal Affairs, Wellington, 1958, p.42.

10. Davin, op cit, p.89.

11. W.B. Thomas, *Dare to be Free*, Allan Wingate, London, 1951, p.15; James McNeish, *Dance of the Peacocks*, Random House, Auckland, 2003, p.185.

12. Hadjipateras & Fafalios, op cit, p.82.

13. D.W. Sinclair, *19 Battalion and Armoured Regiment*, War History Branch, Department of Internal Affairs, 1954, p.140.

14. Henderson, op cit, p.63.

15. Ibid, p.64.

16. Haddon Donald, Interview for 'Freyberg V.C.' series.

17. Henderson, op cit, p.70.

18. Megan Hutching ed., *A Unique Sort of Battle*, HarperCollins, Auckland, 2001, p.156.

19. Davin, op cit, p.143.

20. Beevor, op cit, p.200.

21. Hadjipateras & Fafalios, op cit, p.94.

22. Davin, op cit, p.166.

23. Glyn Harper, *Kippenberger*, HarperCollins, Auckland, 1997, p.93.

24. Mcleod, op cit, p.40.

25. Peter McIntyre, *The Painted Years*, A.H. & A.W. Reed, Wellington, 1962, pp.89–99.

26. Archives New Zealand, DA 52/10/10, Hargest, J. Extracts from Letters and Diary, 8 February 1941 to 25 June 1941.

27. Davin, op cit, p.132.

28. Ibid, p.124.

29. Tony Simpson, *Operation Mercury*, Hodder & Stoughton, London, 1981, p.174. Unfortunately, Laurie Barber and John Tonkin-Covell repeat this unlikely story in *Freyberg: Churchill's Salamander*, as well as the recollection of another soldier who stated that around 6 p.m. he took a request to Davin concerning the state of the 22nd Battalion and that Davin's reply was, wrongly, reassuring. In fact, at this point Davin was lying half paralysed at a first-aid post, having been shot earlier in the day, and was in no position to comment on the situation at the airfield. Laurie Barber & John Tonkin-Covell, *Freyberg: Churchill's Salamander*, Century Hutchinson, Auckland, 1989, pp.60–61, 64.

30. Haddon Donald, Interview for 'Freyberg V.C.' series.

31. Henderson, op cit, p.70.

32. Ibid, pp.55–56.

33. Barber & Tonkin-Covell, op cit, p.69.

34. Ibid, pp.72–73.

35. I.McD.G. Stewart, *The Struggle for Crete*, Oxford University Press, London, 1966, p.231.

CHAPTER 5: DAY ONE: RETIMO, HERAKLION AND KASTELLI KISAMOU

1. Laurie Barber & John Tonkin-Covell, *Freyberg: Churchill's Salamander*, Century Hutchinson, Auckland, 1989, p.79.

2. Costas Hadjipateras & Maria Fafalios, *Crete 1941 Eyewitnessed*, Efstathiadis Group, Anixi Attikis, 1989, p.149.

3. Ibid, p.113.

4. Antony Beevor, *Crete: The Battle and the Resistance*, Penguin, London, 1992, p.139.

5. Ibid, p.138.

6. Hadjipateras & Fafalios, op cit, p.107.

7. Geoffrey Cox, *A Tale of Two Battles*, William Kimber, London, 1987, p.75.

8. *Documents Relating to New Zealand's Participation in the Second World War 1939–45*, Vol. I, War History Branch, Department of Internal Affairs, Wellington, 1949, p.299.

9. Paul Freyberg, *Bernard Freyberg V.C.*, Hodder & Stoughton, London, 1991, p.273.

10. D.M. Davin, *Crete*, War History Branch, Department of Internal Affairs, Wellington, 1953, p.467.

11. Cox, op cit, p.84.

CHAPTER 6: DESPERATE MEASURES

1. I.McD.G. Stewart, *The Struggle for Crete*, Oxford University Press, London, 1966, pp.253–254.

2. Laurie Barber & John Tonkin-Covell, *Freyberg: Churchill's Salamander*, Century Hutchinson, Auckland, 1989, p.80.

3. Costas Hadjipateras & Maria Fafalios, *Crete 1941 Eyewitnessed*, Efstathiadis Group, Anixi Attikis, 1989, p.72.

4. Matthew Wright, *Battle for Crete*, Reed, Auckland, 2003, p.65.

5. D.M. Davin, *Crete*, War History Branch, Department of Internal Affairs, Wellington, 1953, p.134.

6. Jim Henderson, *22 Battalion*, War History Branch, Department of Internal Affairs, Wellington, 1958, p.71.

7. Stewart, op cit, p.108.

8. Archives New Zealand, IA 181/32/2 Part 1, 25 March 1949.

9. Barber & Tonkin-Covell, op cit, p.31.

10. Ibid, p.32.

11. Antony Beevor, *Crete: The Battle and the Resistance*, Penguin, London, 1992, pp.349–351, for the Ultra signals sent before 20 May.

12. Ibid, p.93. See also Kippenberger's remarks in Denis McLean, *Howard Kippenberger*, Random House, Auckland, 2008, p.306.
13. Beevor, op cit, p.157.
14. Ibid; Matthew Wright, *Freyberg's War*, Penguin, Auckland, 2005, p.68.
15. Beevor, op cit, p.157.
16. Gavin Long, *Australia in the War of 1939–1945: Greece, Crete and Syria,* Australian War Museum, Canberra, 1953, pp.234–235.
17. Hadjipateras & Fafalios, op cit, p. 39.
18. Ibid, pp.122–123.
19. Callum Macdonald, *The Lost Battle: Crete 1941,* Macmillan, London, 1995, p.240.
20. Hadjipateras & Fafalios, op cit, p.124.
21. Ibid, pp.138–139.
22. Alan Clark, *The Fall of Crete*, Anthony Blond, London, 1962, pp.120–121.
23. Geoffrey Cox, *A Tale of Two Battles*, William Kimber, London, 1987, pp.82–83.

CHAPTER 7: TOO LITTLE, TOO LATE

1. Archives New Zealand, IA 181/32/2 Part 1, letter 9 February 1950. The officers were Lieutenant Colonel Gentry and Major Burrows.
2. Roy Farran, *Winged Dagger*, Collins, London, 1947, p.94.
3. D.M. Davin, *Crete*, War History Branch, Department of Internal Affairs, Wellington, 1953, p.216.
4. Ben Porter, Interview for 'Freyberg V.C.' series.
5. Davin, op cit, p.220.
6. Davin, op cit, p.472.
7. Ibid.
8. Davin, op cit, p.229. Freyberg's battle diary described this as a 'fantastic story'; Laurie Barber & John Tonkin-Covell, *Freyberg: Churchill's Salamander*, Century Hutchinson, Auckland, 1989, p.90.
9. Davin, op cit, p.226.
10. Ibid, p.239.
11. I.McD.G. Stewart, *The Struggle for Crete*, Oxford University Press, London, 1966, p.482.
12. Costas Hadjipateras & Maria Fafalios, *Crete 1941 Eyewitnessed*, Efstathiadis Group, Anixi Attikis, 1989, p.184.

CHAPTER 8: A FIGHTING WITHDRAWAL

1. D.M. Davin, *Crete*, War History Branch, Department of Internal Affairs, Wellington, 1953, p.251.
2. W.B. Thomas, *Dare to be Free*, Allan Wingate, London, 1951, p.16.
3. Geoffrey Cox, *A Tale of Two Battles*, William Kimber, London, 1987, p.88; Davin, op cit, p.353.
4. John McLeod, *Myth and Reality*, Reed Methuen, Auckland, 1986, p.35.
5. Laurie Barber & John Tonkin-Covell, *Freyberg: Churchill's Salamander*, Century Hutchinson, Auckland, 1989, p.95.
6. Costas Hadjipateras & Maria Fafalios, *Crete 1941 Eyewitnessed*, Efstathiadis Group, Anixi Attikis, 1989, p.188.
7. W.D. Dawson, *18 Battalion and Armoured Regiment,* War History Branch, Department of Internal Affairs, Wellington, p.153.
8. Denis McLean, *Howard Kippenberger*, Random House, Auckland, 2008, p.179.
9. Howard Kippenberger, *Infantry Brigadier*, Oxford University Press, London, 1949, p.66.
10. Davin, op cit, p.313.
11. Thomas, op cit, p.314.
12. Angus Ross, *23 Battalion*, War History Branch, Department of Internal Affairs, Wellington, 1959, p.81.
13. Barber & Tonkin-Covell, op cit, p.102.
14. J.F. Cody, *28 (Maori) Battalion*, War History Branch, Department of Internal Affairs, Wellington, 1956, p.116.
15. Barber & Tonkin-Covell, op cit, p.104.
16. I.McD.G. Stewart, *The Struggle for Crete*, Oxford University Press, London, 1966, p.426.
17. Antony Beevor, *Crete: The Battle and the Resistance*, Penguin, London, 1992, p.198.
18. Davin, op cit, p.375; Stewart, op cit, p.424.
19. J.F. Cody, *21 Battalion*, War History Branch, Department of Internal Affairs, Wellington, 1953, pp.101–102.
20. Hadjipateras & Fafalios, op cit, p.199.
21. *Documents Relating to New Zealand's Participation in the Second World War 1939–45*, Vol. I, op cit, p.308.
22. Ibid, pp.308–309.

CHAPTER 9: HE WHO FIGHTS AND RUNS AWAY

1. '. . . lives to fight another day.' Jack Griffith recalled Freyberg quoting this saying when discussing the evacuation of his forces from Crete, Interview for 'Freyberg V.C.' series.
2. Paul Freyberg, *Bernard Freyberg V.C.*, Hodder & Stoughton, London, 1991, pp.309–310.
3. Antony Beevor, *Crete: The Battle and the Resistance*, Penguin, London, 1992, p.200; Matthew Wright, *Battle for Crete*, Reed, Auckland, 2003, p.90.
4. Angus Ross, *23 Battalion*, War History Branch, Department of Internal Affairs, Wellington, 1959, p.91.
5. Baron von der Heydte, *Daedalus Returned*, Hutchinson, London, 1958, pp.162–163.
6. Gavin Long, *Australia in the War of 1939–1945: Greece, Crete and Syria*, Australian War Museum, Canberra, 1953, p.292.
7. Beevor, op cit, p.216.
8. Ross, op cit, p.89.
9. D.M. Davin, *Crete*, War History Branch, Department of Internal Affairs, Wellington, 1953, p.404.
10. W.D. Dawson, *18 Battalion and Armoured Regiment*, War History Branch, Department of Internal Affairs, Wellington, p.159.
11. J.F. Cody, *28 (Maori) Battalion*, War History Branch, Department of Internal Affairs, Wellington, 1956, p.125.
12. Geoffrey Cox, *A Tale of Two Battles*, William Kimber, London, 1987, p.97; Roy Ferguson, Interview for 'Freyberg V.C.' series.
13. Denis McLean, *Howard Kippenberger*, Random House, Auckland, 2008, p.188.
14. Roy Ferguson, Interview for 'Freyberg V.C.' series.

15. Gerald Hensley, *Beyond the Battlefield*, Penguin, Auckland, 2009, p.122.
16. Wright, op cit, p.100.
17. Freyberg, op cit, p.312.
18. J.F. Cody, *21 Battalion*, War History Branch, Department of Internal Affairs, Wellington, 1953, p.107.
19. Ross, op cit, p.93.
20. Davin, op cit, p.454.
21. Costas Hadjipateras & Maria Fafalios, *Crete 1941 Eyewitnessed*, Efstathiadis Group, Anixi Attikis, 1989, p.280.
22. Davin, op cit, pp.486–488, 521; Beevor, op cit, p.230; David Thomas, *Crete 1941: The Battle at Sea*, Cassell, London, 2003, pp.214–217; Hellenic Army General Staff, *An Abridged History of the Greek-Italian and Greek-German War 1940–1941 (Land Operations)*, Army History Directorate, Athens, 1997, p.294.

CHAPTER 10: RETRIBUTION AND RECRIMINATION

1. Alan Clark, *The Fall of Crete*, Anthony Blond, London, 1962, p.58.
2. Antony Beevor, *Crete: The Battle and the Resistance*, Penguin, London, 1992, p.236.
3. Costas Hadjipateras & Maria Fafalios, *Crete 1941 Eyewitnessed*, Efstathiadis Group, Anixi Attikis, 1989, p.296.
4. Ibid, p.288–289.
5. Paul Freyberg, *Bernard Freyberg V.C.*, Hodder & Stoughton, London, 1991, p.313.
6. Archives New Zealand, DA 52/10/10, Hargest, J. Extracts from Letters and Diary, 8 February 1941 to 25 June 1941.
7. Ibid.
8. Laurie Barber & John Tonkin-Covell, *Freyberg: Churchill's Salamander*, Century Hutchinson, Auckland, 1989, pp.112–113.
9. Guy Salisbury-Jones, Interview for 'Freyberg V.C.' series.
10. Archives New Zealand, DA 52/10/10, op cit.
11. Freyberg, op cit, p.315.
12. *Documents Relating to New Zealand's Participation in the Second World War 1939–45*, Vol. I, op cit, p.323.
13. John McLeod, *Myth and Reality*, Reed Methuen, Auckland, 1986, p.176.
14. Gerald Hensley, *Beyond the Battlefield*, Penguin, Auckland, 2009, p.132.
15. Freyberg, op cit, p.334.
16. Sir John White, Interview for 'Freyberg V.C.' series.
17. Jim Henderson, *22 Battalion*, War History Branch, Department of Internal Affairs, Wellington, 1958, p.83.
18. W.E. Murphy, *The Relief of Tobruk*, War History Branch, Department of Internal Affairs, Wellington, 1961, p.342.
19. Freyberg, op cit, p.329.
20. Denis McLean, *Howard Kippenberger*, Random House, Auckland, 2008, p.290.
21. Ibid.
22. D.M. Davin, *Crete*, War History Branch, Department of Internal Affairs, Wellington, 1953, p.523.
23. W.G. Stevens, *Freyberg, V.C. The Man*, A.H. & A.W. Reed, Wellington, 1965, p.127.
24. Beevor, op cit, pp.229–230.

25. Davin, op cit, p.464.
26. Law Reports of Trials of War Criminals, Vol. IV, 24. Trial of Kurt Student; Wikipedia: Razing of Kandanos; Axis History Forum: Generaloberst Kurt Student. Accessed March 2010.

CHAPTER 11: A RECKONING

1. *Documents Relating to New Zealand's Participation in the Second World War 1939–45*, Vol. I, op cit, pp.306, 308.
2. Ibid, p.323.
3. Matthew Wright, *Battle for Crete*, Reed, Auckland, 2003, pp.111–113.
4. Archives New Zealand, IA 181/32/2 Part 2, letter 12 January 1951.
5. John McLeod, *Myth and Reality*, Reed Methuen, Auckland, 1986, p.16.
6. Archives New Zealand, IA 181/32/2 Part 2, Comments on Draft History, pp.194–256.
7. *The Dominion*, 9, 27 and 30 April 2001.
8. Archives New Zealand, IA 181/32/2 Part 2, Comments on Draft History, pp.135–193. Kippenberger compared Andrew's actions, unfavourably, with Colonel Malone's defence of Chunuk Bair during the Gallipoli campaign in August 1915.
9. Archives New Zealand, IA 181/32/2 Part 2, Comments on Draft History, pp.194–256.
10. Glyn Harper, *Kippenberger*, HarperCollins, Auckland, 1997, p.93.
11. Alan Clark, *The Fall of Crete*, Anthony Blond, London, 1962, p.103.
12. I.McD.G. Stewart, *The Struggle for Crete*, Oxford University Press, London, 1966, p.429.
13. Archives New Zealand, IA 181/32/2 Part 1, 5 December 1949, Appendix II.
14. B.H. Liddell Hart, *The Other Side of the Hill*, Cassell, London, 1951, p.241.
15. Hugh Trevor-Roper, *Hitler's Table Talk*, Phoenix Press, London, 1953, p.466.
16. Paul Freyberg, *Bernard Freyberg V.C.*, Hodder & Stoughton, London, 1991, p.335.
17. Charles Upham, Interview for 'Freyberg V.C.' series.
18. Costas Hadjipateras & Maria Fafalios, *Crete 1941 Eyewitnessed*, Efstathiadis Group, Anixi Attikis, 1989, p.213.
19. Research Institute for Military History ed., *Germany and the Second World War*, Vol. 3, Oxford University Press, London, 1995, p.552.
20. Antony Beevor, *Crete: The Battle and the Resistance*, Penguin, London, 1992, p.230.
21. Hadjipateras & Fafalios, op cit, p.319.

INDEX

Page numbers in **bold** refer to illustrations.